FLOYD CLYMER'S MOTORCYCLIST'S LIBRARY

BOOK OF THE B.S.A.

A COMPLETE GUIDE FOR OWNERS
AND PROSPECTIVE PURCHASERS
OF B.S.A. MACHINES

DEALING WITH EVERY PHASE OF MOTOR-CYCLING FROM THE REGISTRATION TO SELLING OF THE MACHINE SECOND-HAND, AND INCLUDING CHAPTERS ON DRIVING, TOURING, LEGAL MATTERS, INSURANCE, OVERHAULING

BY

F. J. CAMM

EDITOR "PRACTICAL MOTORI."

SEVENTH EDITION
1935

ANNOUNCEMENT

By special arrangement with the original publishers of this book, Sir Isaac Pitman & Son, Ltd., of London, England, we have secured the exclusive publishing rights for this book, as well as all others in THE MOTORCYCLIST'S LIBRARY.

Included in THE MOTORCYCLIST'S LIBRARY are complete instruction manuals covering the care and operation of respective motorcycles and engines; valuable data on speed tuning, and thrilling accounts of motorcycle race events. See listing of available titles elsewhere in this edition.

We consider it a privilege to be able to offer so many fine titles to our customers.

FLOYD CLYMER
Publisher of Books Pertaining to Automobiles and Motorcycles

2125 W. PICO ST.   LOS ANGELES 6, CALIF.

INTRODUCTION

Welcome to the world of digital publishing ~ the book you now hold in your hand, while unchanged from the original edition, was printed using the latest state of the art digital technology. The advent of print-on-demand has forever changed the publishing process, never has information been so accessible and it is our hope that this book serves your informational needs for years to come. If this is your first exposure to digital publishing, we hope that you are pleased with the results. Many more titles of interest to the classic automobile and motorcycle enthusiast, collector and restorer are available via our website at www.VelocePress.com. We hope that you find this title as interesting as we do.

NOTE FROM THE PUBLISHER

The information presented is true and complete to the best of our knowledge. All recommendations are made without any guarantees on the part of the author or the publisher, who also disclaim all liability incurred with the use of this information.

TRADEMARKS

We recognize that some words, model names and designations, for example, mentioned herein are the property of the trademark holder. We use them for identification purposes only. This is not an official publication.

INFORMATION ON THE USE OF THIS PUBLICATION

This manual is an invaluable resource for the classic motorcycle enthusiast and a "must have" for owners interested in performing their own maintenance. However, in today's information age we are constantly subject to changes in common practice, new technology, availability of improved materials and increased awareness of chemical toxicity. As such, it is advised that the user consult with an experienced professional prior to undertaking any procedure described herein. While every care has been taken to ensure correctness of information, it is obviously not possible to guarantee complete freedom from errors or omissions or to accept liability arising from such errors or omissions. Therefore, any individual that uses the information contained within, or elects to perform or participate in do-it-yourself repairs or modifications acknowledges that there is a risk factor involved and that the publisher or its associates cannot be held responsible for personal injury or property damage resulting from the use of the information or the outcome of such procedures.

WARNING!

One final word of advice, this publication is intended to be used as a reference guide, and when in doubt the reader should consult with a qualified technician.

PREFACE
TO SEVENTH EDITION

THE Seventh Edition of this book goes to press at a time when considerable changes are being made in motoring laws. The wide powers conferred on the Minister of Transport enables him to make regulations of a temporary nature, and it is therefore quite possible that by the time this edition reaches the public many new regulations will have been made which are not herein treated. Unfortunately, this is unavoidable, and entirely beyond the control of an author or his publishers. I shall, of course, be glad to advise readers as in the past if they address a letter to me c/o the Publishers and enclose a stamped and addressed envelope.

Readers should particularly bear in mind the new speed limit of 30 miles an hour in built-up areas—which are legally defined as any area in which lamp-posts for street lighting appear at intervals of not more than 200 yards.

Noteworthy changes in the 1935 range of B.S.A. motor-cycles include the reversion to the upright cylinder with the single cylinder models, the introduction of the 4·98 h.p. twin, and quickly detachable wheels and hinged rear mudguards. The 1·49 h.p. O.H.V. Model is a fascinating little machine. The reduction by 25 per cent of the road fund tax has made motor-cycling easily the cheapest, most economical and rapid means of transport.

May I accord my thanks to the many hundreds of readers of previous editions who have written expressing their appreciation of this Manual which is an Annual!

F. J. CAMM.

CONTENTS

CHAP.		PAGE
	PREFACE	
I.	THE B.S.A. RANGE	1
II.	REGISTRATION, DRIVING LICENCE, AND EQUIPMENT	23
III.	DRIVING	35
IV.	HOW THE ENGINE WORKS	56
V.	MECHANICAL DETAILS OF THE B.S.A.	67
VI.	OVERHAULING	91
VII.	TOURING	123
VIII.	FAULTS: THEIR LOCATION AND REMEDY	130
IX.	LEGAL MATTERS	140
X.	BUYING AND SELLING AN OLD MOUNT	144
XI.	THE 1936 MODELS	147
	USEFUL INFORMATION	153
	INDEX	156

B.S.A.
officially recommend
AEROSHELL
LUBRICATING OIL

BOOK OF THE B.S.A.

CHAPTER I

THE B.S.A. RANGE

FOURTEEN models comprise the 1935 range of motor-cycles (excluding the Three-wheeler, which is also described in this chapter).* Four of them are side valve models, and the remainder are overhead models. They range in power from 1·49 h.p. to 9·86 h.p. and in price from £31 7s. 6d. to £75. There is thus a model to suit every pocket and every purpose, and the extreme reliability of the B.S.A. range coupled with their unrivalled service for spares makes it one of the leading ranges of the day. In this Seventh Edition brief specifications of the complete range are given in this chapter, together with illustrations of the various mounts. It will be noted that there is a fair choice of extras, although in many cases horns and lighting are included as part of the standard equipment.

The 1·49 h.p. O.H.V. Model X35-0. Single cylinder O.H.V. engine, 149 c.c. (52 by 70 mm.). Lubrication by mechanical pump incorporating sight feed and accessible adjustment on timing cover. Roller big-end bearings, ball bearings for drive-side of mainshaft. Aluminium alloy piston. Detachable cylinder head. Enclosed O.H.V. gear. Amal carburettor. Improved exhaust silencing. Twist grips 5s. extra. B.S.A. pattern controls and twist grips 7s. 6d. extra.

TRANSMISSION. Front chain ½ in. by ·305 in., specially lubricated. Rear chain ½ in. by ·305 in. Dry plate clutch. B.S.A. three-speed gearbox with inclined gear lever on tank. Gear ratios 7·1, 12·4, 19·8.

FRAME. Diamond type of great strength. B.S.A. front forks with adjustable shock absorbers. Central spring-up stand. Dunlop 3·00-19 tyres. Brakes 5½ in. diameter, front operated by right handlebar lever, rear by right toe-pedal, both quickly adjustable. Adjustable handlebar. Rear portion of mudguard detachable. Saddle tank holds 2 gallons of petrol and 3 pints of oil. Knee-grips fitted.

* See also *Book of the B.S.A. Three Wheeler* (Jelley). ISBN 9781588501851

EQUIPMENT. Lucas M.L. 6-volt lighting set driven from timing gear, with handlebar headlamp dipper control; high-frequency

FIG. 1. THE 1·49 H.P. O.H.V. MODEL

electric horn; licence holder. Detachable carrier. Dunlop pillion seat in place of carrier 8s. 6d. extra.

FINISH. Black and chromium. Green tank with improved side panels. Chromium tank with green panels 15s. extra.

FIG. 2. THE 2·49 H.P. S.V. MODEL

The 2·49 h.p. S.V. Model B35-1. Side valve, single cylinder engine, 249 c.c. (63 by 80 mm.). Lubrication by mechanical pump incorporating sight feed and accessible adjustment on timing cover. Roller big-end bearing with improved lubrication, ball bearings for drive-side of mainshaft. Aluminium alloy piston.

Detachable cylinder head. Enclosed valves with inlet valve lubrication. Amal carburettor. Improved exhaust silencing. Twist grips 5s. extra. B.S.A. pattern controls and twist grips 7s. 6d. extra.

TRANSMISSION. Front chain ½ in. by ·305 in., specially lubricated. Engine shaft cush drive. Rear chain ½ in. by ·305 in. Dry plate clutch. B.S.A. three-speed gearbox with inclined gear lever on tank. Gear ratios, 6·6, 9·8, 14·5.

FRAME. Diamond type of great strength. B.S.A. front forks with adjustable shock absorbers. Central spring-up stand.

FIG. 3. THE 2·49 H.P. O.H.V. MODEL

Dunlop 3·00-10 tyres. Brakes 5½ in. diameter, front operated by right handlebar lever, rear by right toe-pedal, both quickly adjustable. Adjustable handlebar. Rear portion of mudguard detachable. Saddle tank holds 2 gallons of petrol and 3 pints of oil. Knee-grips fitted.

EQUIPMENT. Lucas M.L. 6-volt lighting set driven from timing gear, with handlebar headlamp dipper control, high-frequency electric horn, licence holder. Detachable carrier, Dunlop pillion seat in place of carrier, 8s. 6d. extra. Large Dunlop saddle. Complete tool kit and inflator. Lucas Magdyno lighting set, 30s. extra.

FINISH. Black and chromium. Green tank with improved side panels. Chromium tank with green side panels, 15s. extra.

The 2·49 h.p. O.H.V. Model B35-2. Single cylinder O.H.V. engine, 249 c.c. (63 by 80 mm.). Lubrication by mechanical pump incorporating sight feed and accessible adjustment on timing cover. Roller big end, with improved lubrication, ball bearings for drive-side of mainshaft. Aluminium alloy piston. Detachable cylinder head. Enclosed O.H.V. gear with inlet valve lubrication. Amal carburettor. Improved exhaust silencing.

TRANSMISSION. Front chain ½ in. by ·305 in. lubricated from engine. Engine-shaft cush drive. Rear chain ½ in. by ·305 in. Dry plate clutch. B.S.A. three-speed gearbox with inclined gear lever on tank. Gear ratios, 6·2, 9.3, 13·6.

FRAME. Diamond type of great strength. B.S.A. front forks with quickly adjustable shock absorbers. Central spring-up stand. Dunlop 3·00–19 tyres. Brakes 5½ in. diameter, front operated by right handlebar lever, rear by right toe-pedal, both quickly adjustable. Rear portion of mudguard detachable. Saddle tank holds 2 gallons of petrol and 3 pints of oil. Knee-grips fitted.

EQUIPMENT. B.S.A. adjustable handlebar with special controls, including twist grips for throttle and ignition, and ratchet front brake. Detachable carrier. Large Dunlop saddle. Complete tool kit and inflator. Lucas M.L. 6-volt lighting set, driven from timing gear, with handlebar headlamp dipper control; high-frequency electric horn. Licence holder. Lucas Magdyno lighting set, 30s. extra.

FINISH. Black and chromium. Chromium tank with green side panels of improved design.

The 2·49 h.p. O.H.V. De Luxe Model B35-3.

Single cylinder O.H.V. engine, 249 c.c. (63 by 80 mm.). High efficiency single port cylinder head. Dry sump lubrication by twin gear pump to roller big end and overhead rocker gear. Enclosed inlet valve mechanism. Lubricated inlet valve guide. Oil returns to tank (3¼ pints) under saddle. Tell-tale on timing cover. Ball and roller bearings for drive-side mainshaft, ball bearing timing side. Gear driven magdyno, Amal carburettor, and large capacity silencer, giving subdued exhaust note.

TRANSMISSION. Engine-shaft cush drive. Front chain ½ in. by ·305 in., lubricated by oil well in chain case, automatically replenished from the engine. Rear chain ½ in. by ·305 in. Dry plate clutch. B.S.A. four-speed gearbox with inclined gear lever on tank. Enclosed foot gear change with indicator for gear positions, 17s. 6d. extra. Screw adjustment for front chain. Gear ratios, 6·4, 8·4, 13·2, 19·1.

FRAME. Cradle frame of great strength. B.S.A. front forks with quickly adjustable shock absorbers and steering damper. Saddle tank of new design (2¾ gallons), knee-grips. Two-level petrol tap. Spring-up rear stand and quick action prop stand. Lifting handle on hinged rear guard. Quickly detachable rear wheel. Dunlop tyres, 3·25–19. Brakes 7 in. rear, operated by left toe-pedal, front $5\frac{1}{2}$ in., operated by lever on handlebar. Quick release for front brake.

EQUIPMENT. B.S.A. handlebar with special controls, including twist grips for throttle and ignition and ratchet front brake. Large Dunlop saddle. Approved pillion seat or detachable carrier, 12s. extra. Twin metal toolboxes on mudguard with complete tool kit in a leather case. Inflator. Lucas 6-volt Magdyno electric

FIG. 4. THE 2·49 H.P. O.H.V. DE LUXE MODEL

lighting. High-frequency electric horn. Anti-vibration battery. Licence holder.

FINISH. Black and chromium. Tank chromium with green panels of new design.

The 3·48 h.p. O.H.V. De Luxe Model R35-4. Single cylinder O.H.V. engine, 348 c.c. (71 by 88 mm.). High efficiency single port cylinder head. Dry sump lubrication by twin gear pump to roller big end and overhead rocker gear. Enclosed inlet valve mechanism. Lubricated inlet valve guide. Oil returns to tank ($3\frac{1}{4}$ pints) under saddle. Tell-tale on timing cover. Ball and roller bearings for drive-side mainshaft, ball bearing timing side. Gear driven magdyno. Amal carburettor. Large capacity silencer giving subdued exhaust note.

TRANSMISSION. Engine-shaft cush drive. Front chain $\frac{1}{2}$ in. by ·305 in., lubricated by oil well in chain case, automatically replenished from engine. Rear chain $\frac{1}{2}$ in. by ·305 in. Dry plate clutch. B.S.A. four-speed gearbox with inclined gear lever on tank. Enclosed foot gear change with indicator for gear positions, 17s. 6d. extra. Screw adjustment for front chain. Gear ratios, 5·8, 7·6, 12, 17·4.

FRAME. Cradle frame of great strength. B.S.A. front forks with quickly adjustable shock absorbers and steering damper. Saddle tank of new design (2¾ gallons), knee-grips. Two-level petrol tap. Spring-up rear wheel. Dunlop tyres, 3·25–19. Brakes 7 in. rear, operated by left toe-pedal, front 5½ in., operated by lever on handlebar. Quick release for front brake.

EQUIPMENT. B.S.A. handlebar with special controls, including twist grips for throttle and ignition and ratchet front brake. Large Dunlop saddle. Approved pillion seat or detachable carrier, 12s. extra. Twin metal toolboxes on mudguard with complete tool kit in a leather case. Inflator. Lucas 6-volt Magdyno

FIG. 5. THE 3·48 H.P. O.H.V. DE LUXE MODEL

electric lighting. High-frequency electric horn. Anti-vibration battery. Licence holder.

FINISH. Black and chromium. Tank chromium with green side panels of new design.

The 3·48 h.p. O.H.V. Blue Star Model R35-5. Single cylinder 2-port O.H.V. engine, 348 c.c. (71 by 88 mm.). Lubrication from gear pump to double roller big end. Oil sump (3 pints) and crankcase cast in one unit. Enclosed inlet valve mechanism. Lubricated inlet valve guide. Oil control with safety device. Pressure gauge in tank and dip-stick on filler plug. Roller bearing mainshaft. High compression aluminium alloy piston. Special cams, gear driven magdyno, with shield. Sports plug. Amal pump carburettor. Improved exhaust silencing.

TRANSMISSION. Engine-shaft cush drive. Front chain ½ in. by ·305 in., lubricated by oil well in improved chain case. Rear chain ⅝ in. by ¼ in., with lower run guard. Dry plate clutch; B.S.A.

four-speed gearbox with enclosed foot control and indicator for gear positions. Hand gear change optional, screw adjustment for front chain. Gear ratios, 6·0, 7·9, 12·4, 18·0 solo; 6·7, 8·8, 13·8, 20 sidecar.

FRAME. Duplex cradle with forged steel backbone and integral sidecar lugs. New B.S.A. front forks with improved action. Stronger links and new design shock absorber. Saddle tank of improved design (2¾ gallons), with knee-grips. Two-level petrol tap. Spring-up rear stand and quick action prop stand. Lifting handle on hinged rear guard. Quickly detachable rear wheel. Dunlop tyres, 3·25–19. Front 3·00–20 optional. Brakes 7 in.

FIG. 6. THE 3·48 H.P. O.H.V. BLUE STAR MODEL

diameter, front, with quick release, operated by lever on handlebar. Rear operated by left toe-pedal, both quickly adjustable. Upswept exhaust pipes. Steering damper.

EQUIPMENT. B.S.A. flexibly mounted handlebar with special controls, including twist grips for the throttle and ignition, and ratchet lever for the front brake. A spring seat saddle is fitted. Detachable carrier, or approved pillion seat if specified. Twin metal toolboxes on mudguard with complete tool kit in a leather case. Lucas 6-volt Magdyno electric lighting with large headlamp, tank instrument panel, and Altette electric horn. Anti-vibration battery. Licence holder. Provision is made for pillion footrests. Valanced front guard, 7s. 6d. extra.

FINISH. Black and chromium, including rims. Tank chromium with green side panels of improved design. Special finish to the crankcase and gearbox.

The 4·99 h.p. S.V. Model W35-6. Single cylinder S.V. engine,

499 c.c. (85 by 88 mm.). Enclosed side valves. Lubricated inlet valve guide. Lubrication from gear pump to double roller big end. Oil sump (3 pints) and crankcase cast in one unit. Oil control with safety device. Pressure gauge in tank and dip-stick on filler plug. Roller bearing mainshaft. Aluminium alloy piston. Gear driven magdyno. Detachable head. Amal carburettor, and improved exhaust silencing.

TRANSMISSION. Engine-shaft cush drive. Front chain ½ in. by ·305 in., lubricated by oil well in an improved chain case, automatically replenished from the engine. Rear chain ⅝ in. by ¼ in. Dry plate clutch. B.S.A. four-speed gearbox with screw adjust-

FIG. 7. THE 4·99 H.P. S.V. MODEL

ment for the front chain and inclined gear lever on the tank. Gear ratios, 5·3, 7·0, 10·9, 15·8 solo, and 5·9, 7·8, 12·2, and 17·6 sidecar.

FRAME. Duplex cradle with forged steel backbone and integral sidecar lugs. New B.S.A. front forks with improved action. Stronger links are fitted and new design shock absorber. The saddle tank is of improved design (2¾ gallons) with knee-grips. Two-level petrol tap. Spring-up rear stand and quick action prop stand. Lifting handle on hinged rear guard. Dunlop tyres 3·25–19. Brakes 7 in. diameter, front, with quick release, operated by lever on the handlebar, the rear operated by the right toe-pedal, and both are quickly adjustable. Steering damper.

EQUIPMENT. B.S.A. flexibly mounted handlebar with special controls, including twist grips for the throttle and ignition and ratchet lever for the front brake. Spring seat saddle. Detachable carrier fitted, or approved pillion seat if specified. Metal toolbox on chainstay with complete tool kit in a leather case. Inflator.

THE B.S.A. RANGE

Lucas 6-volt Magdyno electric lighting with large headlamp, tank instrument panel, and Altette electric horn. Anti-vibration battery. Licence holder. Provision is made for pillion footrests.
FINISH. Black and chromium. Tank chromium with green side panels of improved design.

The 4·99 h.p. O.H.V. Model W35-7. Single cylinder 2-port O.H.V. engine, 499 c.c. (85 by 88 mm.). Lubrication from gear pump to double roller big end. Oil sump (3 pints) and crankcase cast in one unit. Enclosed inlet valve mechanism. Lubricated inlet valve guide. Oil control with safety device. Pressure gauge

FIG. 8. THE 4·99 H.P. O.H.V. MODEL

in tank and dip-stick on filler plug. Roller bearing mainshaft. Aluminium alloy piston. Gear driven magdyno, with shield. Amal carburettor. Improved exhaust silencing.
TRANSMISSION. Engine-shaft cush drive. Front chain ½ in. by ·305 in., lubricated by oil well in improved chain case, automatically replenished from engine. Special gland plate at rear of chain case. Rear chain ⅝ in. by ¼ in. with lower run guard. Dry plate clutch. B.S.A. four-speed gearbox with screw adjustment for front chain and inclined gear lever on tank. Gear ratios, 4·8, 6·4, 9·9, 14·3, 11·5, and 16·7 sidecar.
FRAME. Duplex cradle with forged steel backbone and integral sidecar lugs. New B.S.A. front forks with improved action. Stronger links and new design shock absorber. Saddle tank of improved design (2¾ gallons), with knee-grips. Two-level petrol tap. Spring-up rear stand and quick prop stand. Lifting handle on hinged rear guard. Quickly detachable rear wheel. Dunlop tyres, 3·25–19. Brakes 7 in. diameter, front, with quick release,

operated by lever on handlebar. Rear operated by left toe-pedal, both quickly adjustable. Steering damper.

EQUIPMENT. B.S.A. flexibly mounted handlebar with special controls, including twist grips for throttle and ignition, and ratchet lever for front brake. Spring seat saddle. Detachable carrier fitted, or approved pillion seat if specified. Metal toolbox on chainstay with large complete tool kit in a leather case. Inflator. Lucas 6-volt Magdyno electric lighting with large headlamp, tank instrument panel, and Altette electric horn. Anti-vibration battery. Licence holder. Provision is made for pillion footrests.

FINISH. Black and chromium. Tank chromium with green side

FIG. 9. THE 4·99 H.P. O.H.V. BLUE STAR MODEL

panels of improved design. Special finish to the crankcase and gearbox.

The 4·99 h.p. O.H.V. Blue Star Model W35-8. Single cylinder 2-port O.H.V. engine, 499 c.c. (85 by 88 mm.). Lubrication from gear pump to double roller big end. Oil sump (3 pints) and crankcase cast in one unit. Enclosed inlet valve mechanism. Lubricated inlet valve guide. Oil control with safety device. Pressure gauge in the tank and dip-stick on the filler plug. Roller bearing mainshaft. High compression aluminium alloy piston. Special cams; gear driven magdyno, with shield. A sports plug is fitted, and Amal carburettor. Improved exhaust silencing.

TRANSMISSION. Engine-shaft cush drive. Front chain $\frac{1}{2}$ in. by ·305 in., lubricated by oil well in improved chain case, automatically replenished from the engine. Special gland plate at rear of chain case. Rear chain $\frac{5}{8}$ in. by $\frac{1}{4}$ in. with lower run guard.

Dry plate clutch. B.S.A. four-speed gearbox with enclosed foot control and indicator for gear positions. Hand gear change optional, screw adjustment for front chain. Gear ratios, 4·8, 6·4, 9·9, 14·3 solo; 5·6, 7·4, 11·5, and 16·7 sidecar.

FRAME. Duplex cradle with forged steel backbone and integral sidecar lugs. New B.S.A. front forks with improved action. Stronger links and new design shock absorber. Saddle tank of improved design (2¾ gallons) with knee-grips. Two level petrol tap. Spring-up rear stand and quick prop action. Lifting handle on hinged rear guard. Quickly detachable rear wheel. Dunlop tyres, 3·25-19. Front 3·00-20 optional. Brakes 7 in. diameter, front, with quick release, operated by lever on handlebar. Rear operated by left toe-pedal, both being quickly adjustable. Upswept exhaust pipes. Steering damper.

EQUIPMENT. B.S.A. flexibly mounted handlebar with special controls, including twist grips for throttle and ignition and ratchet lever for front brake. Spring seat saddle. Detachable carrier fitted, or approved pillion seat if specified. Twin metal toolboxes on mudguard with complete tool kit in a leather case. Inflator. Lucas 6-volt Magdyno electric lighting with large headlamp, tank instrument panel, and Altette electric horn. Anti-vibration battery. Licence holder. Provision for pillion footrests. Valanced front guard for 7s. 6d. extra.

FINISH. Black and chromium, including rims. Tank chromium with green side panels of improved design. Special finish to the crankcase and gearbox.

The 4·99 h.p. O.H.V. Special Model W35-9.

Single cylinder 2-port O.H.V. engine, 499 c.c. (85 by 88 mm.). Specially built and tested. Lubrication from gear pump to double roller big end. Oil sump (3 pints) and crankcase cast in one unit. Enclosed inlet valve mechanism with lubrication for guide. Oil control with safety device. Pressure gauge in tank and dip-stick on filler plug. Roller bearing mainshaft. Downdraught cylinder head. Special racing piston. Special valves and springs; special cams, rockers and rocker box. Gear driven magdyno, with shield. Super-sports 14 mm. plug, special T.T. carburettor.

TRANSMISSION. Engine-shaft cush drive. Front chain ½ in. by ·305 in., fully lubricated by oil well in an improved chain case, automatically replenished from the engine. Special gland plate at the rear of chain case. Rear chain ⅝ in. by ¼ in. with lower run guard. Dry plate clutch. B.S.A. four-speed gearbox with enclosed foot control, and indicator for gear positions; hand gear change optional; screw adjustment for the front chain. Gear ratios, 4·8, 6·4, 9·9, 14·3 solo, and 5·6, 7·4, 11·5, and 16·7 sidecar.

FRAME. Duplex cradle with forged steel backbone. New B.S.A.

front forks with improved action. Stronger links and new design shock absorber. Saddle tank (2¾ gallons), with knee-grips. Two-level petrol tap. Spring-up rear stand and quick action prop stand. Lifting handle on hinged rear guard. Quickly detachable rear wheel. Dunlop tyres, 3·25–19 rear, 3·00–20 front. Brakes 7 in. diameter, front, with quick release, operated by lever on handlebar, rear by left toe-pedal, and both quickly adjustable. Special silencing system. Steering damper.

EQUIPMENT. B.S.A. flexibly mounted handlebar with special controls. Binks racing twist grip throttle. Ratchet lever for

FIG. 10. THE 4·99 H.P. O.H.V. SPECIAL MODEL

front brake. Adjustable spring seat saddle. Rear mudguard pad. Metal toolbox on chainstay with complete tool kit in a leather case. Inflator. Lucas 6-volt Magdyno electric lighting with a large headlamp, tank instrument panel, and Altette electric horn. Anti-vibration battery. Licence holder. Provision is made for pillion footrests.

FINISH. Black and chromium, including the rims. Tank chromium with green side panels of improved design.

The 5·95 h.p. S.V. Model M35-10.
Single cylinder S.V. engine, 595 c.c. (85 by 105 mm.). Enclosed side valves. Lubricated inlet valve guide. Lubrication from gear pump to double roller big end. Oil sump (3 pints) and crankcase cast in one unit. Pressure gauge in tank and dip-stick on the filler bracket. Mainshaft on ball and roller bearings. Aluminium alloy piston. Gear driven magdyno, and Amal carburettor.

TRANSMISSION. Engine-shaft cush drive. Front chain ½ in. by ·305 in., lubricated by oil well in the chain case, automatically replenished from the engine. Special gland plate at the rear of chain case. Rear chain ⅜ in. by ⅜ in. with lower run guard. Dry plate clutch. B.S.A. four-speed gearbox with screw adjustment for front chain. Gear ratios, 5·1, 6·7, 10·5, 15·2 solo, and 5·9, 7·8, 12·1, and 17·6. Enclosed foot gear change, 17s. 6d. extra.

FRAME. Duplex cradle with forged steel backbone and integral sidecar lugs. B.S.A. front forks with adjustable shock absorbers. Saddle tank (2¾ gallons), with knee-grips. Spring-up rear stand. Lifting handle on hinged rear guard. Dunlop tyres, 3·25–19.

FIG. 11. THE 5·95 H.P. S.V. MODEL

Brakes 7 in. by 1¾ in. diameter, front, with quick release, operated by lever on the handlebar, rear by the right toe-pedal, and both are quickly adjustable. Quickly detachable rear wheel.

EQUIPMENT. B.S.A. flexibly mounted handlebar with special controls, including twist grips for throttle and ignition and ratchet lever for front brake. Spring seat saddle. Detachable carrier fitted, or approved pillion seat if specified. Metal toolbox on chainstay with complete tool kit in leather case. Inflator. Lucas 6-volt Magdyno electric lighting with large headlamp, tank instrument panel, and Altette electric horn. Anti-vibration battery. Licence holder.

FINISH. Black and chromium. Tank chromium with green side panels of improved design.

The 5·95 h.p. O.H.V. Model M35-11. Single cylinder, 2-port O.H.V. engine, 595 c.c. (85 by 105 mm.). Lubricated inlet valve guide. Lubrication from gear pump to double roller big end and cams. Oil sump (3 pints) and crankcase cast in one unit. Pressure gauge in tank and dip-stick on filler bracket. Mainshaft on ball and roller bearings. Aluminium alloy piston. Gear driven magdyno, with shield. Amal carburettor.

TRANSMISSION. Engine-shaft cush drive. Front chain ½ in. by ·305 in., lubricated by oil well in the chain case, automatically replenished from the engine. Special gland plate at the rear of chain case. Rear chain ⅝ in. by ⅜ in. with lower run guard. Dry plate clutch. B.S.A. four-speed gearbox with screw adjustment

FIG. 12. THE 5·95 H.P. O.H.V. MODEL

for the front chain. Gear ratios, 4·8, 6·4, 9·9, 14·3 solo, and 5·6, 7·4, 11·5, and 16·7 sidecar. Enclosed foot gear change, 17s. 6d. extra.

FRAME. Duplex cradle with forged steel backbone and integral sidecar lugs. B.S.A. front forks with quickly adjustable shock absorbers. Saddle tank (2¾ gallons), with knee-grips. Two-level petrol tap. Spring-up rear stand. Lifting handle on hinged rear guard. Dunlop tyres, 3·25–19. Brakes 7 in. diameter, front, with quick release, operated by lever on handlebar, rear by the right toe-pedal, and both quickly adjustable. Quickly detachable rear wheel. Steering damper.

EQUIPMENT. B.S.A. flexibly mounted handlebar with special controls, including twist grips for the throttle and ignition. Ratchet lever for the front brake. Spring seat saddle. Detachable carrier fitted, or approved pillion seat if specified. Metal toolbox on chainstay with complete tool kit in a leather case. Inflator. Lucas 6-volt Magneto electric lighting with large headlamp, tank instrument panel, and Altette electric horn. Anti-vibration battery. Licence.

FINISH. Black and chromium. Tank chromium with green

side panels of improved design. Special finish to the crankcase and gearbox.

The 4·98 h.p. O.H.V. Vee-twin Model J35-12. Vee-twin cylinder O.H.V. engine, 498 c.c. (63 by 80 mm.). Dry sump lubrication by double gear pump to double roller big ends and overhead rocker gear. Oil returns to tank (5 pints) under saddle. Oil control with safety device. Pressure gauge in tank. Enclosed

Fig. 13. The 4·98 h.p. O.H.V. Vee-Twin Model

inlet valve mechanism. Mainshaft on ball and roller bearings (double on drive side). Aluminium alloy pistons. Improved exhaust silencing. Gear driven racing magdyno with shield.

TRANSMISSION. Engine-shaft cush drive. Front chain ½ in. by ·305 in., lubricated by oil well in improved chain case, automatically replenished from engine. Special gland plate at rear of chain case. Rear chain ⅝ in. by ¼ in. with lower run guard. Dry plate clutch. B.S.A. four-speed gearbox with enclosed foot control with indicator for gear positions. Hand gear change optional; screw adjustment for front chain. Gear ratios, 4·8, 6·4, 9·9, 14·3 solo, and 6·25, 8·25, and 18·6 sidecar.

FRAME. Duplex cradle with forged steel backbone and integral sidecar lugs. New B.S.A. front forks with improved action. Stronger links and new design shock absorber. Saddle tank holding 3 gallons, with knee-grips. Spring-up rear stand and quick action prop stand. Lifting handle on hinged rear mudguard. Quickly detachable rear wheel. Dunlop tyres, 3·25–19. Brakes 7 in. diameter, front, with quick release, operated by lever on the handlebar, and rear by left toe-pedal, both being quickly adjustable. Steering damper.

EQUIPMENT. B.S.A. flexibly mounted handlebar with special controls, including twist grips for throttle and ignition, ratchet lever for the front brake. Spring seat saddle. Approved pillion seat fitted, or detachable carrier if specified. Twin metal toolboxes on the mudguard with a complete tool kit in a leather case. Inflator. Lucas 6-volt Magdyno electric lighting and large headlamp, tank instrument panel, and Altette electric horn. Anti-vibration battery. Licence holder. Provision is made for pillion footrests. and a valanced guard for 7s. 6d. extra.

FINISH. Black and chromium. Tank chromium with green

FIG. 14. THE 9·86 H.P. VEE-TWIN MODEL

side panels of improved design. Special finish to the crankcase and gearbox.

The 9·86 h.p. Vee-twin Model G35-14. Single cylinder S.V. engine, 986 c.c. (80 by 98 mm.). Enclosed side valves. Lubrication by double mechanical pump to front cylinder and double roller big ends. Oil compartment in tank (3½ pints). Roller bearing mainshaft. Aluminium alloy pistons. High efficiency detachable heads. Amal carburettor. Magdyno shield.

TRANSMISSION. Engine-shaft cush drive. Both chains ⅝ in. by ⅜ in., front, lubricated by oil well in the chain case. Special gland plate at the rear of chain case. Lower run rear guard. Dry plate clutch with specially enclosed and lubricated control. B.S.A. three-speed gearbox of increased strength, with adjustment for the front chain. Gear ratios, 4·5, 7·1, 11·4 solo, and 4·7, 7·5, 12·0 sidecar. B.S.A. four-speed gearbox £1 extra.

FRAME. Specially designed for heavy sidecar work. Integral sidecar lugs. B.S.A. front forks with adjustable shock absorbers.

THE B.S.A. RANGE

Saddle tank (3 gallons), with knee-grips. Spring-up rear stand. Lifting handle on hinged rear guard. Dunlop tyres, 4·00–19 or 3·50–21. Brakes 7 in. diameter, front operated by lever on the handlebar, rear by the right heel pedal, and both are quickly adjustable. Quickly detachable and interchangeable wheels. Steering damper.

EQUIPMENT. B.S.A. handlebar with special controls, including twist grips for throttle and ignition. Ratchet lever for front brake. Spring seat saddle. Detachable carrier fitted, or approved pillion seat if specified. Metal toolbox on chainstay with complete kit in a leather case. Inflator. Lucas 6-volt Magdyno electric lighting, large headlamp, tank instrument panel and Altette electric horn. Anti-vibration battery. Licence holder.

FINISH. Black and chromium. Tank chromium with green side panels of improved design.

B.S.A. THREE WHEELERS *

The Standard Model TW35-1. Twin-cylinder engine. Fabric finish body and folding hood with side-screens. A safety glass flat windscreen is fitted. Black enamelled five-lamp set. Hinged locker lid giving access to the rear luggage compartment. Quickly detachable rear guard to facilitate wheel changing. Pneumatic upholstery for seat in leather cloth. All fittings chromium plated. Colour, black and red.

De Luxe Model TW35-2. Twin-cylinder engine. Aluminium panelled body, with cellulose finish. A flat safety glass windscreen and standard folding hood is fitted. V type windscreen and detachable hood to order. Fort Dunlop tyres. Chromium plated five-lamp set. Large diameter tail pipe. Hinged locker lid to give access to the luggage compartment at rear is fitted. Quickly detachable rear guard to facilitate wheel changing. Pneumatic upholstery for seat in leather cloth. Silent double-helical constant mesh gears. Chromium plated fittings. Colours, lavender and grey, dual grey, and black with ivory, blue, red, or green.

The Special Model TW35-9. This is similar to the De Luxe Model but has tuned engine with a special carburettor, spring steering wheel, electric screen-wiper, and combined stop and tail lamp.

The Family De Luxe Model TW35-5. Twin-cylinder engine. Aluminium panelled body, with cellulose finish. Folding hood, with four sidescreens. A safety-glass flat windscreen is fitted.

* See also *Book of the B.S.A. Three Wheeler* (Jelley). ISBN 9781588501851

Fort Dunlop tyres. Chromium plated five-lamp set. Driver's seat is adjustable, and the front passenger's seat is hinged. Pneumatic upholstery for the seat with leather cloth. Silent double-helical constant mesh gears. All fittings chromium plated. Colours, black and blue, dual grey, grey and lavender, and black with ivory, red, or green.

The Four-cylinder Model TW35-10. Four-cylinder engine. Aluminium panelled body, with cellulose finish. Detachable hood with sidescreen, stored in locker. Safety-glass flat windscreen, and electric screen-wiper. $4\frac{1}{2}$ in. Dunlop tyres. A chromium plated five-lamp set. Combined stop and tail lamp. Hinged locker lid to give access to the luggage at the rear. Quickly detachable rear guard to facilitate wheel changing. Pneumatic upholstery for the seat, with leather cloth. Silent double-helical constant mesh gears. All chromium plated fittings. A new design slatted radiator is fitted. The colours are dual grey, grey and lavender, or black with ivory, blue, red, or green.

The Four-cylinder De Luxe TW35-10. Four-cylinder engine. Aluminium panelled body with cutaway doors. Finished in cellulose. Spring steering wheel. Fold-away hood of new design, with sidescreens stored in the locker. Safety-glass folding windscreen with round corners. An electric windscreen-wiper is fitted. $4\frac{1}{2}$ in. Dunlop tyres. Five-lamp set, with chromium plated finish. Combined stop and tail lamp. Hinged locker lid to give access to the luggage compartment at the rear. Detachable rear guard to facilitate wheel changing. Pneumatic upholstery for the seat, with leather cloth. Silent double-helical constant mesh gears. All fittings chromium plated. A new design slatted radiator is fitted. Colours, black and ivory, dual grey or lavender and grey.

THE THREE-WHEELER SPECIFICATION. Twin-cylinder engine. Air-cooled V-twin, 85 by 90 mm., 1021 c.c.; ball and roller mainshaft bearings, roller big ends; and O.H.V. enclosed push rods.

Four-cylinder engine. Water cooled, 60 by 95 mm., 1075 c.c.; ball and roller mainshaft bearings; short large-diameter crankshaft. S.V. enclosed.

GENERAL. Lucas 6-volt coil ignition and lighting; dynamo; starter; automatic advance on four-cylinder, manual on twin; special aluminium alloy pistons; gear type oil pump; sump capacity 1 gallon four-cylinder, 5 pints twin; efficient lubrication system supplying oil under pressure to vital parts; Solex carburettor (self-starter type on four-cylinders).

TRANSMISSION. Multiple large-diameter wet cork clutch; three

THE B.S.A. RANGE

forward speeds and reverse, 5·16 top, 7·75, 16·8, and 20·7 reverse; worm final drive; spur type differential; flexible couplings and metal universal joints in axle shafts.

BRAKES. Internal expanding of ample size; pedal operates all brakes with special compensation for rear; hand lever on rear only.

FRAME AND SUSPENSION. Channel section steel frame of great strength; independent springing, four quarter elliptic front springs; frame side members converge to a bracket at the end of a strong steel tube; quarter elliptic rear spring inside tube; grease gun lubrication to all the chassis parts; quickly detachable and interchangeable wheels. Spare wheel complete.

Overall length, 11 ft. 2 in. Overall width, 4 ft. 10 in. Wheelbase, 7 ft. 6½ in. Track, 4 ft. 2 in.

EQUIPMENT. Speedometer, electric horn, oil gauge, ammeter, screenwiper. A full kit of tools, including jack, wheel brace, tyre pump, and grease gun. A licence holder is fitted.

LUGGAGE SPACE. In addition to providing roomy seating accommodation for the driver and passenger, the B.S.A. Threewheeler has ample space for luggage, except in the Family model, where the space is used for children's seats. It is not just a case of strapping suitcases to an exposed luggage grid—the luggage, which could consist of two large suitcases or several smaller ones, stows away in the roomy tail, under complete cover.

Luggage can be loaded either by raising the locker lid (which can be locked when closed) or by moving the hinged seat-back forward.

REMOVAL OF THE REAR WHEEL. While it is quite possible to jack up and remove the rear wheel from underneath the body, a quickly detachable top guard is now fitted inside the locker space to enable this operation to be carried out from above (except on the Family model).

By removing the four wing nuts holding the wheel-guard in position, the guard can be removed. The jack can then be placed in position and the four wheel nuts removed from above.

B.S.A. SIDECARS

Special Sports Model 21-44. This model is suitable for the 3·48 h.p. O.H.V. Blue Star models. The chassis is of scientific triangular construction with immensely strong rear axle tube. It has universal type connections adaptable to any 1935 B.S.A. motor-cycle suitable for sidecar work; new Cee spring rear suspension, silentbloc oil-less bearings without shackles, and two helical springs at the front.

The body is designed on modern lines, and this new model meets the requirements of sporting appearance and low cost. The construction is simple and rigid, and the wind resistance low. It is cellulose finished in two shades of blue with blue upholstery, or green and ivory with green upholstery, and the upholstery lifts to give access to capacious locker space at the rear. It is fitted with a sports windscreen, apron and chromium plated semi-

Fig. 15. The Special Sports Sidecar Model

circular hand rail, also electric sidecar lamp. The price of this model is £17. Tax 15s.

The Medium Tourer Model 21-20. This model is intended for the 3·48 h.p. O.H.V. Blue Star models. The chassis is of triangular construction with immensely strong rear axle tube. It has universal connections adaptable to any B.S.A. motor-cycle suitable for sidecar work, new Cee spring rear suspension, silentbloc oil-less bearings without shackles, and two helical springs at the front.

The body is cellulose finished in green and ivory, with green upholstery, arm rests, lock-up luggage compartment behind the fixed back seat, apron and windscreen, also electric sidecar lamp. This model costs £17. Tax 15s.

The Large Tourer Model 21-40. This model is suitable for the 4·99 h.p. S.V. range. The chassis is of scientific triangular construction with immensely strong rear axle tube giving great

THE B.S.A. RANGE

strength without unnecessary weight. It has universal type connections adaptable to any 1935 B.S.A. motor cycle which is suitable for sidecar work; new Cee spring rear suspension, silentbloc oil-less bearings without shackles, and two helical springs at the front.

The body is of large capacity, giving ample accommodation,

Fig. 16. The Launch Sidecar Model

and having pleasing modern lines. The riding position is low, so that the passenger is comfortably seated and well protected. A commodious luggage locker is fitted behind the seat back, the locker lid being shaped to blend with the body contour; electric sidecar lamp; rear luggage rail and folding hood extra. It is cellulose finished in two shades of blue, with blue upholstery. The price of this is £20. Tax 15s.

The Launch Model 21-42. This model is suitable for the 3·48 h.p. O.H.V. Blue Star range. The chassis is of scientific construction with immensely strong rear axle tube, giving great strength without unnecessary weight. It has universal type connections adaptable to any 1935 B.S.A. motor-cycle which is suitable for sidecar work; Cee spring rear suspension, silentbloc oil-less bearings without shackles, and two helical springs at the front.

The body is an improved model of the well-known B.S.A. Launch, with deeper sides affording greater comfort and improving the general appearance. A chromium plated deck rail is fitted, complete weather protection provided by a three-panel safety-glass windscreen, with chromium plated frame, and detachable hood. It is cellulose finished in maroon and ivory with maroon upholstery, and an electric sidecar lamp is fitted. This model costs £22 10s. Tax 15s.

The Heavy Tourer Models 6B-6 and 6C6. These models are intended for motor-cycles from 5·95 h.p. The chassis is of triangular construction, with four-point connection. It has universal

Fig. 16A. The Heavy Tourer Sidecar Model

attachments as with the light touring chassis; transverse semi-elliptic spring at the rear, helical spring at front, and spring shackles lubricated with grease gun. Model No. 6B6 can be fitted with $5\frac{1}{2}$ in. diameter brake at an extra charge of £2. Model 6C6 has a sprung wheel, and this can be fitted with 7 in. diameter brake at an extra charge of £2 12s. 6d.

The body is designed on ample lines to give the maximum room and comfort. It is coach finished in B.S.A. green with upholstery to match, arm rests, spring-seat cushion, tool locker under seat, lock-up luggage compartment in the back, constructed to accommodate a child's seat. The seat and squab is 15s. extra. Waterproof apron and windscreen, also electric sidecar lamp are also fitted. The 6B6 model costs £20, and the 6C6 model £25 5s. Tax 15s.

CHAPTER II

REGISTRATION, DRIVING LICENCE, AND EQUIPMENT

IN this chapter, the writer pre-supposes that the reader, having selected the mount to suit his inclinations, now turns to the question of the necessary legal formalities and requirements to be satisfied before the machine may be taken on the road.

The New Driving Licence Regulations. The new Driving Licence Regulations which came into force on 1st April, 1935, affect every new motorist who applied for his first Driving Licence on or after 1st April, 1934. The important clauses are here summarized for the convenience of new motor-cyclists and car drivers. The Road Traffic Act of 1934 revokes the Motor Vehicles (Driving Licences) Regulations of 1930. The important point is that all motorists whose licences fall within the period mentioned above, and all new motorists who in the future apply for driving licences, will have to undergo a driving test. Applications for the grant of a driving licence will be received and dealt with any time within two months before the date on which the grant of the licence is to take effect. A provisional licence will be granted for purposes of the test. The driving licence fee remains unchanged, but a further fee of 7s. 6d. has to be paid to cover the cost of the test.

Disqualification. No person will be supplied with a driving licence who suffers from epilepsy, any form of mental disorder or mental defect as a result of which the subject is certified or certifiable as to be placed under statutory supervision; liability to sudden attacks of disabling giddiness or fainting, or inability to read at a distance of 25 yards in good daylight (with the aid of glasses if worn) a series of six letters and figures in white on a black ground of the same size as those used for the index plate of motor cars. In order to pass the driving tests, the motorist must satisfy the authority that he is fully conversant with the contents of the Highway Code, that he is able, unaided, to start the engine of the vehicle, move away straight ahead or at an angle; overtake, meet, or cross the path of other vehicles and take an appropriate course, turn right-hand and left-hand corners correctly, stop the vehicle in an emergency, and bring his vehicle to rest at an appropriate part of the road; drive the vehicle backwards (this applies only to cars) and enter a limited opening to the right or to the left; cause the vehicle to face in the opposite direction by the use of forward and reverse gears; give by hand (except in the case of a disabled driver) and by mechanical means (if fitted to the vehicle), in a clear and unmistakable manner, appropriate signals at appropriate times to indicate his intended actions. The reversing clause above does not apply to vehicles not equipped with means for reversing.

Correct Signalling. He must act promptly on all signals by traffic signs, traffic controllers, and other road users. The intending driver must demonstrate that he is capable of driving a motor vehicle without danger to other users of the road. Tests may be conducted by supervising examiners appointed by the Ministry of Transport, by the Board of Admiralty, Army Council, or the Air Council. Any person may apply to the Ministry for permission to conduct tests of persons in his employment if the number of drivers employed exceeds 250, and proper arrangements are made for conduct of the tests stated; proper records of such tests must be kept. Any person desiring to pass the tests should apply to the Supervising Examiner to the traffic area in which he resides. Any driver failing to pass the tests may re-submit after a month. The vehicle, while being driven by a person who is the holder of a provisional licence shall display on the front and back of the vehicle the letter L (learner).

The Driving Licence. This licence must be in the possession of all drivers of motor vehicles when driving, and it must be produced when the request is made by a police officer. The mere possession of the licence, be it noted, does not discharge liability, for it must be carried whilst driving the vehicle. *It may not be lent* to any person for the purpose of driving the owner's machine. A declaration of physical fitness must be made at the time of application. It is procurable from the local Borough or County Council office, and it costs 5s. per year, the year counting from the date on which the licence is issued until the corresponding date of the subsequent year. The forms of application for licences have been simplified, and in the case of renewal without alteration of circumstances nothing is now required beyond the applicant's name and address and licence number. No person under the age of 14 may apply for a driving licence. The driving licence *must be signed by the owner.* It is an offence not to do so.

Registration and Tax. All motor-cycles must be registered at the local Borough or County Council office, and if the machine is to be used on the public roads a tax, according to the cubic capacity of the engine, must be paid. This basis of taxation only applies for new machines registered since 1st January, 1933. In the case of a machine registered before that date the owner may pay the tax according to the old system of taxation if such taxation amounts to less than the new system. If, however, it is to his advantage to renew under the new system he may do so.

It will be seen that the licence may be taken out annually, quarterly, or part yearly, as detailed later on. For the purpose of the law, the term *weight unladen* is taken to mean the machine in its running condition, and does not include the tool kit, petrol, accumulators, or water, but it does include headlamp and generator (whether acetylene or electric), horn, and the rear lamp and their connections. The licence (a circular label on which is entered details of machine, date, and amount of tax paid) must be exhibited in a conspicuous position on the near-side (left-hand side when seated on the saddle), and be carried in a weather-proof holder with transparent front so as clearly to be visible by daylight to a person standing at the near-side of the vehicle. Only *two* positions are sanctioned by the authorities: on the near side of the handlebar or on the near-side of the combination.

FORM OF PROVISIONAL LICENCE

No.....................

......................................County (Borough) (Town) Council.

ROAD TRAFFIC ACT, 1930: PROVISIONAL DRIVER'S LICENCE

....

....

of ....

....

is hereby licensed to drive a..

from...19....... until ....

19........ inclusive, subject to the condition that the licence shall only be used by the licensee when under the supervision of a person who has held a driving licence for at least two years who, except in the case of a motor-cycle or invalid carriage, shall be present in the vehicle with the holder of this licence.

(Address of Authority)...

Ordinary signature of licensee..

APPLICATION FOR TEST

The Supervising Examiner (Driving Tests)

....

....

I enclose crossed cheque/or crossed postal order/or money order for 7s. 6d. Please arrange for me to undergo driving test under Section 6 of the Road Traffic Act, 1934.

I desire to be tested at the nearest convenient centre to............................

Name in full (Block Capitals)..
(State Mr., Mrs., or Miss, etc.)

Signature ....

Address ....

Date..

ROAD TRAFFIC ACTS, 1930 AND 1934
Application for a Licence to Drive a Motor Vehicle
A. APPLICATION

I apply for $\dfrac{\text{a provisional (3 months)}}{\text{an annual}}$ licence for the period commencing ....to enable me to drive—

- (a) Motor vehicles of any class or description.
- (b) Motor cars and motor cycles only.
- (c) Motor cycles only.
- (d) Invalid carriages only.
- (e) Motor vehicles of special type (other than invalid carriages) constructed or adapted for use by a person with some physical disability.

B. PARTICULARS TO BE FURNISHED BY APPLICANT

1. Surname
2. Full Christian Names
3. Address of permanent residence in Great Britain
    If applicant has no permanent residence in Great Britain, name and address of agent through whom applicant may be traced.
4. Is applicant (a) under 21 years of age?
    .... (b) under 17 years of age?
    .... (c) under 16 years of age?........
5. Particulars of last licence issued to the applicant.

6. (1) Is the applicant entitled to a licence free from endorsements?
    (2) If the answer to the above is in the negative, give full particulars of every conviction which is required to be endorsed on the licence.

TAX PAYABLE ON THE CUBIC CENTIMETRE BASIS
As from 1st January, 1933

Cubic Capacity of Engine	Annual licences expiring on 31st December	Quarterly licences expiring on 24th March, 30th June, 30th Sept. or 31st December
	Duty. £ s. d.	Duty. £ s. d.
Where the cylinder capacity of the engine does not exceed 150 cubic centimetres .	12 –	3 4
Where the cylinder capacity of the engine exceeds 150 cubic centimetres but does not exceed 250 cubic centimetres . .	1 2 6	6 3
Where the cylinder capacity of the engine exceeds 250 cubic centimetres .	2 5 –	12 5
When sidecar is drawn	4 – –	1 2

REGISTRATION, DRIVING LICENCE, ETC.

Surrender Value. Every licence now has a surrender value; for details apply to the issuing council.

Renewal Before Expiry of Old Licence. A licence may be renewed as early as fourteen days before the expiration of the old licence, and it is advised that advantage be taken of this arrangement.

Exceptions to Renewal at a Post Office. Licences are renewable at the principal money order post offices, except in the following cases: First licences for vehicles not already registered; licences subject to rebate on pre-1913 engines; renewal of licences which have expired more than fourteen days previously; annual licences where the last licences were quarterly, and vice versa; licences for vehicles which have changed ownership since the last licences were issued; in cases where the registered owners of the vehicle have changed their addresses, or where any particulars of the vehicles have been changed since the last licences were issued; applications for the renewal of licences where page 7 of the relative registration book is filled up; trade licences.

Replacing a Lost Book. If by any chance the registration book has been mislaid or lost, then the licensing authority, upon payment of a fee of 5s., will issue a fresh registration book.

If the licence itself has been lost or has become illegible through rain or sun, then the registration book must be immediately returned to be replaced. To ride a motor-cycle with an illegible licence is an offence for which the rider can be convicted and fined. A duplicate can be obtained from the registration authority, but the fee of 5s. will again be demanded unless it is possible to satisfy the authority that the illegibility or fading is not due to any neglect or carelessness.

Regarding the Registration Book. Upon the first issue of the registration book sign your name in the top space provided on page 3. Keep the book in a safe place, not on the vehicle. If you lose the book, you may have trouble and delay in renewing the licence or in disposing of the vehicle; and you should report the loss at once to your registration authority.

If the particulars on page 6 of the book are not correct, inform the registration authority at once.

If you make any change in your vehicle which affects the particulars on page 6 you must at once inform your registration authority and send the book to them. It is an offence not to notify any change of the registration particulars. You must at the same time send the licence when the alteration affects any of the particulars thereon. If the alteration made increases the amount of licence duty payable, you should send a cheque or postal order for the amount of the additional duty.

Renewal of Licence. When your licence expires, if the vehicle has not changed hands since the licence was issued, get a renewal form (R.F. 1A) from your registration authority or from a money order post office, and fill it in. You should then send it to the registration authority or take it to a principal post office in the area of your registration authority, together with the proper duty, when you will get the registration book back, with a new licence. Where renewal is effected at a post office, the old licence must be surrendered at the time of application; in other cases it must be destroyed on expiry. If the last licence was not taken out by you, the vehicle must be fully declared on the appropriate declaration form before a new licence can be obtained.

If the licence is not renewed owing to the non-use of the vehicle, you must retain this registration book and produce it to the registration authority when you apply at a subsequent date for another licence for the same vehicle. When a vehicle is broken up, destroyed, or sent permanently out of Great Britain, the registration book must be surrendered to your registration authority.

Change of Address. If you change your permanent address, at once put your name and new address in Block Capitals in the first vacant " CHANGE " space on page 3 (or 4, if 3 is filled), sign your name below it and post the book to the registration authority whose address is given on page 2 of the registration book.

Transfer of Vehicle. On transferring the vehicle to another person, you must hand over this book to the person acquiring the vehicle. At the same time you must notify in writing (either by letter or on the form mentioned below) the registration authority, whose address is given on page 2, that the vehicle has been handed over, and the notification must contain the following information: The index mark and number of the vehicle; the make and class of vehicle; and the name and address of the person to whom the vehicle was handed over.

A form (R.F. 70) may be obtained for this purpose from any money order post office.

A person acquiring a second-hand vehicle and intending to use it upon the public roads (otherwise than under a Trade Licence) must, as soon as he acquires it, fill up the first vacant " CHANGE " space on page 3 (or 4, if 3 is filled), giving his full name, address, and usual signature, and post this book to the registration authority whose address is given on page 2 of the book. The registration will then be transferred to his name.

Dealers Who Buy to Sell Again. If the person acquiring the vehicle does not intend to use it upon the public roads (otherwise than under a Trade Licence) but to dispose of it to a third party, he need not send in the book or fill in a " CHANGE " space. He must, however, as soon as he acquires the vehicle, notify in writing the registration authority, whose address is given on page

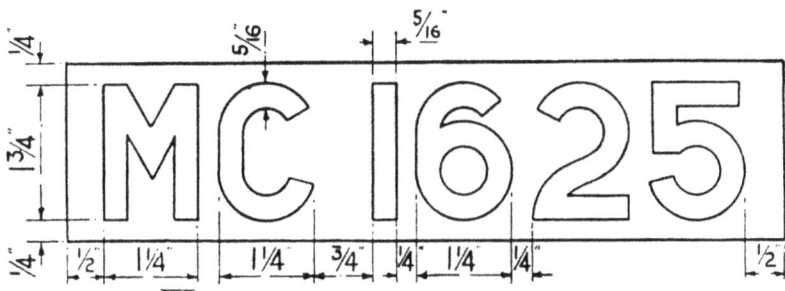

FIG. 17. FRONT NUMBER PLATE DIMENSIONS

2 of the book, that he holds the vehicle but does not intend to use it on the public roads. He must also comply with the instruction given above, on transferring the vehicle to another person. (The procedure outlined in this paragraph is designed to meet the case of dealers and other persons who do not intend to use the vehicle but to dispose of it.)

Part-year Licences. Motor-cycle licences can now be taken out for any number of months, varying from four to eleven, and expiring on 31st December, at one-twelfth the annual rate of duty for each month of the currency of the licence, plus a surcharge.

A typical example of the operation of the part-year licensing scheme is found in the case of a motor-cyclist desirous of taking out a licence for a motor-cycle from 1st June to the end of the year. For a machine over 150 c.c. but less than 250 c.c. the tax on which would be £1 2s. 6d. per annum, the licence duty payable for the seven months is 13s. 10d.

Although this part-year licensing scheme is limited in its scope in that the shortest period allowed is four months, motor-cyclists desirous of laying up their machines during the tail end of the season may do so by surrendering their licences and obtaining a rebate on the unexpired portion. By this means a refund can be obtained for each complete month of the period of the

Area	If you live within the borders of the following Counties	Apply to
NORTHERN	CUMBERLAND, DURHAM, NORTHUMBERLAND AND WESTMORLAND.	The Supervising Examiner (Driving Tests), Ministry of Transport, Low Bridge, 160 Pilgrim Street, Newcastle-on-Tyne 1.
YORKSHIRE	YORKSHIRE.	The Supervising Examiner (Driving Tests), Ministry of Transport, Weetwood Chambers, Albion Street, Leeds 1.
NORTH WESTERN	ANGLESEY, CAERNARVON, CHESHIRE, DENBIGH, FLINT, LANCASHIRE, MERIONETH AND MONTGOMERY.	The Supervising Examiner (Driving Tests), Ministry of Transport, Arkwright House, Parsonage Gardens, Deansgate, Manchester 3.
WEST MIDLAND	HEREFORD, SHROPSHIRE, STAFFORD, WARWICK AND WORCESTER.	The Supervising Examiner (Driving Tests), Ministry of Transport, Unitas House, 24 Livery Street, Birmingham 3.
EAST MIDLAND	BUCKS, DERBY, LEICESTER, LINCOLN, NORTHAMPTON, NOTTINGHAM, OXFORD AND RUTLAND.	The Supervising Examiner (Driving Tests), Ministry of Transport, Grosvenor House, Friar Lane, Nottingham.
EASTERN	BEDFORD, CAMBRIDGE, HUNTINGDON, NORFOLK, SOKE OF PETERBOROUGH, EAST AND WEST SUFFOLK.	The Supervising Examiner (Driving Tests), Ministry of Transport, Sidney House, Sidney Street, Cambridge.
SOUTH WALES	BRECHNOCK, CARDIGAN, CARMARTHEN, GLAMORGAN, MONMOUTH, PEMBROKE, RADNOR.	The Supervising Examiner (Driving Tests), Ministry of Transport, Graham Buildings, Newport Road, Cardiff.
WESTERN	GLOUCESTER, SOMERSET, WILTSHIRE, DORSET, CORNWALL, DEVON.	The Supervising Examiner (Driving Tests), Ministry of Transport, St. Stephens Chambers, Baldwin Street, Bristol 1.
METROPOLITAN AND SOUTH EASTERN	LONDON, KENT, MIDDLESEX, ESSEX, SURREY, BERKSHIRE, HERTFORD, EAST AND WEST SUSSEX, HAMPSHIRE, ISLE OF WIGHT.	The Supervising Examiner (Driving Tests), Ministry of Transport, Romney House, Marsham Street, Westminster, S.W.1.
NORTHERN SCOTLAND	ABERDEEN, ANGUS, BANFF, CAITHNESS, CLACKMANNAN, FIFE, INVERNESS, KINCARDINE, KINROSS, MORAY, NAIRN, PERTH, ROSS AND CROMARTY, SUTHERLAND, ZETLAND, ORKNEY.	The Supervising Examiner (Driving Tests), Ministry of Transport, Crown Mansions, 41¾, Union Street, Aberdeen.
SOUTHERN SCOTLAND	STIRLING, DUMBARTON, EAST AND WEST LOTHIAN, ARGYLL, RENFREW, MIDLOTHIAN, EAST LANARK, PEEBLES, AYR, SELKIRK, BERWICK, ROXBURGH, DUMFRIES, KIRKCUDBRIGHT, WIGTOWN, BUTE.	The Supervising Examiner (Driving Tests), Ministry of Transport, 46 Palmerston Place, Edinburgh 12.

REGISTRATION, DRIVING LICENCE, ETC.

currency of the licence which is unexpired, the refund being calculated *pro rata* plus a fee of 5s.

Number Plates. This simple item of the equipment is hedged round with restrictions. One must be provided at the front and rear of the machine, and upon them must be painted the registered numbers which have been assigned to the machine and which are entered on the registration label and also in the registration book. The numbers must conform to the following proportions : Each figure or letter must be $2\frac{1}{2}$ in. by $1\frac{3}{4}$ in. wide, and $\frac{3}{8}$ in. broad at

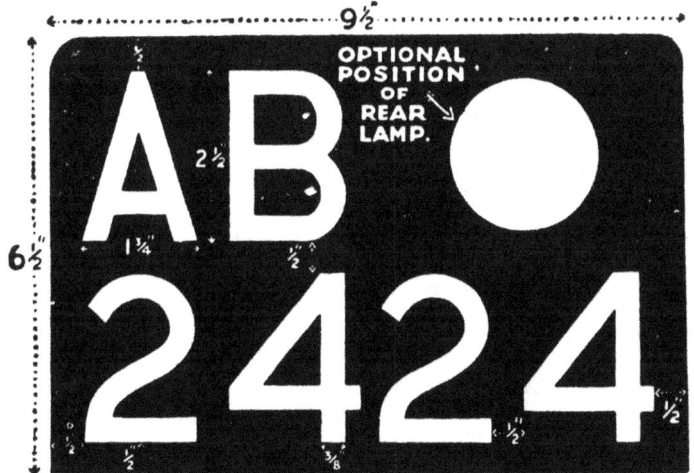

FIG. 18. REAR NUMBER PLATE DIMENSIONS

all parts (see Fig. 18). Between the top and bottom of the letters and the edge of the plate there must be a margin of at least $\frac{1}{2}$ in., with a margin of $\frac{1}{2}$ in. at each side. The letters must be in white on a black ground, and they must not be permitted to become obscured by mud or dust ; nor must the view of them be obstructed by any person or article on the machine.

Lamps. During the period between half-an-hour after sunset and half-an-hour before sunrise it is compulsory to show a white light at the front of the machine, and, in addition, both solo and sidecar machines must show a red light at the rear. During summer time this period is extended by one hour. Red reflectors must not be used. Lamps which remain alight only while the engine is running are illegal unless a stand-by battery is fitted to light the lamps when the engine has stopped. The number plates must be illuminated. If the machine is a combination this also must have a lamp showing white forward, and it must be fixed in such a way that from the front and in conjunction with the headlamp it indicates the extreme width of the vehicle, i.e. on sidecar mudguard.

Audible Warning of Approach. A horn, either of the mechanical or the bulb type, must be fitted so that adequate and audible warning of approach may be given to pedestrians, as well as to the drivers of other vehicles. Preference is given to an electric horn yielding a deep, sonorous note. When a motor vehicle is stationary on the highway, the horn must not be used except when such use is necessary on the grounds of safety. It must not be used in silence zones between the hours of 11.30 p.m. and 7 a.m.

It may be taken that legal matters regarding the machine itself, such as silencing, brakes, etc., have been attended to by the makers, and there is little need to reiterate such regulations here.

FORM OF CERTIFICATE OF PASSING TEST OF COMPETENCE TO DRIVE
ROAD TRAFFIC ACTS, 1930 TO 1934

....

has been examined and has passed the test of competence to drive................. .... prescribed for the purposes of Section 5 of the Road Traffic Act, 1930, or Section 6 of the Road Traffic Act, 1934.

FORM OF STATEMENT OF FAILURE TO PASS TEST OF COMPETENCE TO DRIVE
ROAD TRAFFIC ACTS, 1930 TO 1934

....

has this day been examined and has failed to pass the test of competence to drive prescribed for the purposes of Section 5 of the Road Traffic Act, 1930, or Section 6 of the Road Traffic Act, 1934.

APPLICATION FOR RENEWAL OF LICENCE TO DRIVE A MOTOR VEHICLE

.... I apply for an annual licence in continuation of the accompanying licence No.   and I declare that I am not suffering from any disease or physical disability which would be likely to cause the driving by me of a motor vehicle of the class or description which I was authorized by that licence to drive to be a source of danger to the public. I am aware that it is an offence for a person to use a motor vehicle on public roads unless there is in force a policy of insurance of security against third party risks covering the use by that person of that vehicle.

Strike out if not applicable. Certificate of competence to drive No.   attached hereto.

Signature ....
Address ....
....
Date..

INSURANCE

Under the Road Traffic Act, 1930, motor-cyclists are compelled to insure against third party claims. In addition to the usual policy, or cover note, the insurance company will hand to the owner a certificate of insurance in the prescribed form, and when applying for his motor-cycle licence, the applicant must—by production of the insurance certificate or otherwise—satisfy the Licensing Authority that the necessary cover against third party risks will be in force at the time the motor-cycle licence becomes operative. This certificate of insurance must be carried when driving the machine, and produced upon the request of a police officer.

The Comprehensive Policy. Three classes of insurance policies are issued by the insurance companies for the benefit of motor-cyclists. The first covers, up to an unlimited amount, the owner's legal liability to the public for injury to person and damage to property, and includes all the legal costs incurred with the company's consent (1). Additionally, it covers the cost of legal representation at police courts or inquests in connection with an accident covered by the policy (2), loss or damage caused by fire, lightning, explosion, self-ignition, or by burglary, house-breaking, or theft (3). It also covers loss or damage arising from an accidental explosion, or from wilful or malicious acts, or whilst in transit (4).

Part Cover. Many motor-cyclists, however, prefer to make themselves responsible for the damage caused by a collision, and to meet this, the insurance companies provide a policy appropriately phrased omitting reference to damage arising from accidental collision, etc. Yet other motor-cyclists also prefer to run the fire and theft risks as well, and so a policy is issued which also has no reference to fire and theft.

What the Policy Does not Cover. Solo machines may not carry a pillion passenger unless that clause has been inserted at the request of the insured. Machines used for business purposes may be covered at a special rate according to circumstances. If the motor-cycle is used for racing, pacemaking, trials, or is let out on hire, the policy ceases to operate, nor does it enable a claim to be made for replacements rendered necessary by wear and tear, break-downs, damage to tyres caused by skids, application of brakes, punctures, or bursts.

Insurance Conditions. These are usually simple. The first condition is that the company shall be advised of all accidents immediately. Secondly, that the insured or his agents shall not make any admission of liability to, or negotiate with any third parties, and that he and his agents shall render all reasonable assistance to the company to negotiate, resist, or settle any such claims, the company reserving the right to settle or otherwise deal with such claims at their sole discretion.

The insured shall submit estimates for the repairs of the machine to the company for approval. Generally speaking, reasonable repairs can be authorized by the owner provided no new parts are necessary.

CHAPTER III

DRIVING

IT is worth while giving a few minutes' thought and experiment to the various controls, before actually driving the machine. Pull the machine on to the stand by placing the foot against it as it rests on the ground and pulling the machine back by means of the back fork stays or lifting handle. Do *not* pull it back by means of the saddle, for you may, in the course of time, break a saddle spring by such practice. Now remove the filler cap and fill the petrol tank and also the oil tank or sump. Remove the filler cap from the right-hand end of the gear box, and insert cylinder oil of the grade recommended for the model, until it comes level with the lip of the filler spout and no more can be poured in. Then replace the cap and tighten up with a spanner.

Lubricating the Engine. This is one of the most important points to be remembered in managing a motor-cycle. Whilst it is true that the engine will not run until it has a supply of petrol, it is equally true that it will not run *very long* unless it is kept well supplied with lubricating oil. The friction of the different parts would cause some of the softer metals employed in the bearings to get hot and expand beyond the working point, and the engine would stop suddenly with the bearings or the pistons and cylinder damaged. This is what is technically known as "seizing up." On those models fitted with sight-feed and mechanical pump of the 1935 range (the X35, B35, and B35-2 Models) the first thing to do is to open the supply valve of the lubricating system a few turns, and push down the pump plunger smartly until it remains down. The barrel is then charged and oil flows through the sight-feed. When the plunger rises to the top the pump is empty. Repeat this operation three or four times. The engine will then be sufficiently charged for starting, and the drip may be set at the desired flow by adjustment of the valve. Make certain that the oil tap is "on" if a tap is fitted. Some models are not provided with a tap nor a hand-feed pump.

Before a new machine is run for the first time it is necessary to give the engine a supply of oil. A convenient method (on the 1935 models) of doing this is to remove the sparking plug and turn the engine until the piston is at the bottom of its stroke. Then pour a small quantity of oil (not more than about two teaspoonfuls) into the cylinder through the sparking plug hole. Allow the machine to stand a few minutes before starting up. This will provide the necessary lubrication while the pump is delivering oil from the sump. It is only necessary to oil in this manner when starting a new engine for the first time or after draining the crankcase.

On the sump lubricated models the oil supply is controlled by a valve on the delivery side of the pump, the operation of which is fully described in a later paragraph. This should be studied before the engine is started.

Petrol Supply to the Engine. The next thing to do is to turn on the petrol by turning the lever to the position marked ON. When a priming tap is fitted (it is not fitted to all models) the tap is off when it is pointing vertically downwards. If moved upward towards the front, it allows the petrol to flow along the priming tube; while if moved upward towards the back, it turns the petrol on to the carburettor as explained above.

The Various Controls and Their Purpose. The three main controls to the engine are: (1) the gas supply, (2) the air supply, (3) the spark control for advancing and retarding the spark. There are also one or two minor controls, such as the exhaust lifter, which is used chiefly for starting. These are described in detail later. Another most important control is the clutch. This is simply a device for disconnecting the drive from the gear-box to the rear wheel at will, so that the engine can run without causing any movement of the machine. The gears are controlled by the gear lever, which will be found on the right-hand side of the machine. Anyone who has ridden a three-speed gear bicycle will know why gears are necessary. The low gear is for starting and to make matters easier for the engine when travelling up a steep hill. The second gear is for easing matters on a hill which does not tax the engine to its utmost. The top gear is for normal travelling on the level or up slight inclines and also for travelling down hill. We shall have more to say about the intelligent use of the gears a little later.

Operating the Controls for Starting the Engine. Open the throttle lever (the use of the twist-grip controls fitted to all models except the 1·49 h.p. O.H.V. and 2·49 S.V. Models is dealt with later) a distance equal to about one-third of its full movement. Leave the air lever shut; remember that some controls open outward, and some inward. The air lever is the upper and shorter of the two levers. The lever above the left handlebar is the spark advance lever, which on most of the models advances towards the tank. Set this at about two-thirds advance, that is two-thirds of its total travel from its extreme left-hand position. Now

DRIVING

pull up the exhaust release lever on the left-hand side of the bars as far as it will go. (This is a small trigger lever, and on certain models it is on the right-hand bar.) On those models fitted with twist-grips, the right handlebar twist-grip controls the throttle, and it is opened when turned *towards* the rider. The air control is by means of a short lever mounted on the right handlebar. It opens from left to right. The ignition twist-grip is mounted on the left handlebar. To advance the ignition this is turned towards the rider. See that the gear lever on the right-hand side of the machine is in the neutral position. If the lever should happen to be in another position, raise the exhaust-valve lifter (fitted to the left handlebar), revolve the engine by means of the kick-starter and at the same time push the gear lever into the neutral position. Never attempt to move the gear lever while the engine is stationary.

Before starting the engine see that the oil control on the right-hand side of the machine (on the tank on the 9·86 h.p. models) is open from half to one complete turn. (In the case of the 2·49 h.p. Blue Star Junior, 3·48 h.p., and 4·99 h.p. models the control should be unscrewed as far as it will go.)

Starting the Engine. Everything is now ready for starting the engine, and all that is necessary is to push down the kick-starter pedal smartly with the foot (of course using the exhaust valve lever for a portion of the kick-starter stroke), when the engine should fire at once. Provided the instructions given above as to the setting of the various levers have been carefully followed, the engine should start at the first or second depression of the kick-starter.

Priming the Engine. If the engine feels very stiff when the kick-starter is depressed, it may be advisable to prime the cylinder by removing the plug from the cylinder, and allowing a few drops of petrol to run into it via the priming pipe (if fitted) by turning the petrol tap forwards as explained above. This will free the piston and make it more easy to operate the kick-starter. Be careful not to put too much petrol into the cylinder when priming, and never prime at all unless it is really necessary.

Procedure after Engine has Started. As soon as the engine starts, open the air lever until the engine is firing regularly. It should be noted that the positions given above for the air, throttle, and spark controls are only approximate. A rider can only ascertain by experience the lever positions which enable him to start his own machine most easily. The " sound " and " feel " of a machine which will tell the rider that the engine is running well cannot be imparted by printed instructions.

The Action of the Controls. Let the engine run for a minute or two on the stand, but do not race it. Meanwhile note the results obtained by opening and shutting the throttle and air controls, advancing and retarding the spark, and operating the exhaust valve lifter, so as to become familiar with their operation.

Operating the Clutch and Gears. With the machine still on the stand and the engine running, sit on the saddle and practise operating the clutch and gears. Raise the clutch lever on the outside of the left handlebar, and push the gear lever on the right from the neutral into the low gear position, then allow the clutch to engage by gently releasing the lever held with the left hand. The back wheel will gradually speed up, and by the time the lever has been fully lowered, the wheel will be revolving steadily. To change the gear the clutch should be disengaged and the gear lever smartly moved into the second gear position. Every time the gear is changed the clutch must be disengaged. Do not move the gear lever while the engine is stationary.

THE FIRST SPIN

Next, having returned the gear lever to the neutral position, stand on the left-hand side of the machine, push it gently off the stand, and swing the latter up into position. (On some models a spring-up stand is fitted.) Now mount the machine, (the engine still running), raise the clutch lever (on outside of left handlebar) to its fullest extent, and push the gear lever into *low gear position*. Then engage the clutch by gently and slowly releasing the clutch lever with the left hand at the same time gradually opening the throttle, and the machine will start away smoothly and gather speed. Be careful always to disengage the clutch fully before moving the gear lever from the neutral position. Of course, when the rider is used to the machine, or if the machine has a sidecar, it is not necessary to put it on the stand to start it. The kick-starter can easily be operated by the rider when seated on the saddle.

Changing Gear. As soon as the machine is travelling at a speed of about 10 miles an hour change to second gear, next accelerate to about 20 miles per hour, then change to third gear and finally to top gear. Always declutch when changing gear, and having made the change let the clutch in again slowly. When reducing speed, whether because the machine is climbing a steep hill or for any other cause, do not let the engine labour on top gear. As soon as the engine seems inclined to labour change down into second gear. This is done by lifting the clutch, revving up and pushing the gear lever smartly into the desired position. A similar operation enables the rider to change from second to low gear, if the speed similarly becomes too low for the second gear. Do not be afraid to change to a lower gear if it is thought desirable. The gear box is on the machine for use, and far more harm is done by letting the engine labour and thump unnecessarily on a high gear than by letting it " rev " a little on a lower gear. If very slow running is desired, as for instance when negotiating dense traffic, change into bottom gear and partly disengage the clutch. The clutch is fitted with special friction linings, and cannot be damaged by a reasonable amount of slipping when slow running is required. The point to bear in mind about gear changing is that when *changing up* the engine speed should be reduced, and when *changing down* the engine speed should be increased. This makes silent gear changing easy. The point to aim at is to get the two gear parts which have to engage to revolve at the same speed. Use of the foot gear change is explained on a later page.

The Exhaust-Valve Lifter. Do not control the speed of the engine by operating the exhaust-valve lifter. The speed should always be controlled by the throttle lever, for reasons explained presently, and the exhaust lifter should only be used for starting purposes.

Coasting. When descending hills the clutch may be disengaged and the engine stopped altogether, so that the machine coasts down like a bicycle. After coasting down a hill do not attempt to start the engine by means of the clutch if the low gear is engaged or serious damage may result and you may be thrown over the handlebars. Lift the clutch and engage high gear, open the throttle slightly, and let the clutch in gradually until the engine starts.

Acceleration. It is always wise when driving to avoid violent acceleration, because wheel-spin as well as skids are likely to occur, with decidedly bad effects on the tyres. Always endeavour to take up slowly and evenly, and to accelerate gradually. Whenever possible, regulate the speed by opening or closing the throttle gradually, not suddenly, and use so much air that the engine can be felt to be running under its best conditions. Do not run the engine with the air lever nearly closed for any length of time, otherwise the engine will be liable to overheat.

Instructions for Lubrication of Engines. It will be observed that the oil control knob on the timing cover of all models to which such is fitted, is provided with an extension which projects sideways and which, as it comes into contact with the timing cover, only permits of about five-eighths of one turn of the knob. This is a special feature provided with the object of preventing accidental starvation of oil on the one hand and unnecessary over-lubrication on the other. When the knob is turned in a clockwise direction as far as it will go the oil control is open half a turn, and when it is turned in the other direction as far as it will go the control is open just over one turn. These limits provide a normal range of opening just sufficient for most purposes, but when the machine is well run-in the rider may alter the setting by undoing the screw on the top of the control knob and sliding the knob off its spindle, to which it is coupled by means of splines. If the knob is moved to the next spline forward in an anti-clockwise direction, and the screw on the top is replaced, this will enable the rider to shut his oil control down to about one-third of a turn open in the minimum position and just under one turn in the maximum. In a similar manner the rider may arrange for an increased supply should this be necessary for exceptional circumstances. I recommend, however, that the control setting as given on the machine when it is sent out from the works should not be interfered with during the running-in period. For normal running on most engines a setting of three-quarters of a turn open is about right, but the rider should find by experiment the best setting for his particular machine.

On earlier 5·95 h.p. models the oil control should be opened (turned to the left) from half to one complete turn. This setting is only arbitrary, and the rider should find out for himself the most economical setting consistent with adequate lubrication.

Attention should be paid to the following points in connection with the lubricating system: Check the oil level in the sump regularly by means of the dip-stick. When the level falls to the notch marked "1" the sump should be filled up with a pint of oil. If preferred, the sump can be filled up with a quart of oil when the level falls to the mark "2" on the dipper, or $1\frac{1}{2}$ pints when the level falls to "$1\frac{1}{2}$" on the smaller engines. It is of the utmost importance, however, not to run more than about 20 miles after the oil level has fallen to the mark "2," or "$1\frac{1}{2}$" on the smaller engines. If this distance is exceeded, engine trouble may occur due to lack of lubrication.

Lubrication of the 1·49 h.p., 2·49 h.p. S.V. and 2·49 h.p. O.H.V. Single Port. A simple and efficient lubrication system, with only one external oil pipe has been adopted for these machines. The oil is drawn from a compartment in the petrol tank holding three pints, and delivered to the engine by a pump mounted on the timing cover. A sight-feed is incorporated so that the supply of oil can be readily checked. For normal use the quantity should be adjusted to 14–16 drops per minute. Beyond seeing that there is oil in the tank, and taking care to drain the crankcase every 1,000 miles, little attention is required. After draining give the cylinder a charge of oil, and increase the pump control setting for about 50 miles.

Lubrication (4·98 h.p. Twin). The lubrication system is of the dry sump type. The oil container is mounted on the right, under the saddle, and a gear-type pump, driven from the timing-side mainshaft, draws oil from the tank and delivers it to the big-end bearing through the mainshaft, flywheel, and crank pin. The rocker boxes have separate oil feeds from the relief valve. The other parts are lubricated by splash and the oil, which drains to the bottom of the crankcase, is picked up by the flywheels and returned to a reservoir at the rear of the crankcase by the action of a scraper on the rims of these. The oil is then returned, by a second set of gears in the pump, to the tank. A relief valve is placed in the system to prevent undue load on the pump mechanism.

The oil supply is regulated by a valve on the timing cover. The valve is closed by turning the knob in a clockwise direction and the knob has an extension which, by coming into control with the timing cover, prevents undue rotation in either direction, and therefore makes it difficult to over- or under-lubricate. Further adjustment is obtainable, however, by removing the small screw on the top of the knob and drawing the latter off the splines by which it is connected to the valve spindle. The knob can then be re-set to give a more suitable position. Normally this control is set so that the valve is open from half to just over one complete turn.

The oil flow is indicated by a pressure gauge in the tank. The normal readings are 8–15 lb. per sq. in. when cold, and 3–9 lb. per sq. in. when warm.

The gauge is an indicator of the oil flow, and if the pressure falls much below normal the lubricating system should be examined. First ensure that there is an adequate supply of oil.

9·86 h.p. Twin. The duplex pump is supplied with oil from the compartment in the tank, as with the earlier system. One pipe is used for the supply of both pumps, which are otherwise quite distinct.

The outer pump, with its control at the front, supplies the big-end bearings and other parts. The inner pump, with its control at the rear, supplies the front cylinder. Each control is adjustable, and turning anti-clockwise increases the flow. The oil can be seen flowing in the small chambers visible through the openings at the top of the pump; the chambers are adjacent to their respective controls.

The rate of flow should be adjusted to suit the general conditions of use. For low speed work the supply can be reduced, and for high speed duty it should be increased, but for general purpose a flow of not more than six drops per minute from each sight-feed when ticking over is necessary. This should give 10-12 drops per minute at normal running speeds. During the running-in period (or first 1,000 miles) 25 per cent more oil should be given, and subsequently the quantities should be adjusted to give satisfactory running, as the above figures are arbitrary. The correct setting for any conditions is best determined by experience.

The Running-in Period. The life of the machine will be greatly increased if a speed of not more than 35 miles an hour in top gear is kept to for the first 500 miles, and 25 m.p.h. and 20 m.p.h. and 15 m.p.h. in third, second, and low gears, and a speed not exceeding 40 miles an hour for the next 500 miles. The running-in of a new motor-cycle may be laborious, but it will pay in the long run. Both the crankcase and the oil sump should be drained every 1,000 miles.

The Advance and Retard. Drive with the spark in the position in which the machine accelerates best. A retarded spark causes overheating and excessive petrol consumption.

How to Stop. Having told the reader how to start and ride the machine, it is imperative that he should know how to stop it. The sequence for stopping is as follows : (1) Close throttle ; (2) raise clutch lever ; (3) apply foot-brake and/or hand-brake gradually as found necessary.

Use of the Brakes. What has been said about violent acceleration applies with equal force to the other extreme—violent braking, or deceleration. One of the most frequent causes of skidding is sudden application of the brakes, due to the locking of the wheel. It is this sudden locking which causes a skid, but whether a skid takes place or not, the effect on the tyres is bad.

Adjusting the Brakes. Occasionally it is necessary to adjust the brakes, to compensate for wear. The adjustment should be such that the brake is not rubbing the drum when in the " off " position or power will be lost in overcoming this extra friction. This can be done by placing the machine on the stand, with the gear lever in neutral, spinning the back wheel and adjusting the

DRIVING

brakes until wear is taken up. Nor should the adjustment necessitate a comparatively large movement of the pedal before the brake comes into operation. The rods operating the front brake need attention every now and then, for they are liable to become slack. Do not forget to lubricate the brake fulcrums with the grease-gun, and to roughen the surfaces of the friction linings when they become glazed through constant use.

Oil on the Brakes. The reader is warned not to let oil or grease get on to the brake drums or surfaces, or when the brake is wanted in an emergency it will slip until the oil or grease is squeezed or burnt out.

Greasy Roads. On greasy or wet roads, particularly the new by-pass roads, extreme caution should be observed when the brakes are applied, or skidding is almost certain to result, and the speed of the machine should therefore be regulated according to these road conditions. On a greasy road do not apply the brake to one wheel only; both should be applied. Under these circumstances applying the brakes in a series of jabs often has the desired effect, but in any case, whenever the brakes are used, the clutch should be raised so that the braking effort is not applied to the transmission of the engine.

A good driver uses his brakes as little as possible, and the reader is recommended to cultivate the habit of always allowing plenty of space in which to pull up.

Jab Braking. It should be remembered that if the roads are greasy, it is almost an impossibility to pull up suddenly without experiencing a skid. Special care should, therefore, be exercised when driving under these conditions, and the speed of the machine should be reduced when approaching cross roads. The brake should be applied by jabbing, and not with a steady pressure. This prevents the wheel from becoming locked in one position. The jabs should be steadily, not suddenly, applied.

CONCERNING THE TYRES

The pressure to which the tyres are inflated has an important bearing on the questions of comfort, tyre life, braking efficiency, and life of the machine.

" Hard " Tyres. A tyre inflated too hard does not absorb its share of the road shocks set up by potholes, etc., but passes them on to the springs of the front forks. The rider also will be jolted unnecessarily.

"Soft" Tyres. Dealing with the opposite extreme, tyres inflated to too low a pressure soon wear out, because part of the wear is taken by the "wall," or side, of the tyre, which is not meant to come into contact with the road at all. A "soft" tyre may be comfortable from the rider's point of view, but it may allow the rim to come into contact with the road.

The Correct Tyre Pressure. The tyres should be inflated to the correct pressure as recommended by the tyre manufacturers, and this pressure should be checked once a week by means of a Schrader pressure gauge. Correct tyre pressure is important to ensure maximum tyre mileage.

Sidecar Alignment and its Effect on Tyres and Steering. Sidecar alignment, if defective, has a bad effect on the tyres and steering, causing the tread to wear on one side. If the tyre is noticed to be wearing in this manner, remedy the sidecar alignment and reverse the cover, so that the tyre wear is equalized. See also page 113.

DRIVING A COMBINATION

The actual driving and engine control of a combination does not differ from a solo machine, and the instructions already given need not be repeated here. A solo machine rider will experience a little strangeness with a sidecar outfit, due to the offset drag of the sidecar, which tends to make steering difficult at first by continually edging the machine to the left side of the road and to draw the machine to one side. It is good practice to obtain confidence by taking the machine to the top of a hill and coasting down with free engine, with the foot ready to operate the brake in case of emergency.

The best advice that can be given the new sidecar driver is "go slowly"—particularly on corners. If the rider attempts to take a left-hand turn too rapidly there will be a tendency for the sidecar wheel to rise from the ground owing to the pull of centripetal force. Once the wheel is off the ground steering control is lost, and the outfit turns to the right, and, in some cases overturns. As the rider gains experience, however, he will find that he can corner faster with safety by adopting the following hints—

Making a Left-hand Turn with Sidecar. Brake before the corner, and then accelerate when actually on the bend. In this way the motor-cycle "runs round" the sidecar, the wheel of which acts as a pivot.

Making a Right-hand Turn with Sidecar. Ride up to the corner

DRIVING

fast, and brake when actually on the bend. In this case the sidecar " overruns " the motor-cycle and facilitates the turning action.

After the sidecar has been attached to the motor-cycle for some time, there may be a tendency for the connections to " give " a little, and cause the alignment to be upset. It is advisable, therefore, to check this point from time to time, although the practised combination driver can tell whether the outfit is correctly " lined up " by the manner in which it steers. A pull to the left on an uncambered road is a sure indication that either the machine is leaning inward, or that the sidecar wheel is running outward. Misalignment not only results in bad steering, but it ruins the tyres and imposes undue strains on the motor-cycle frame and the sidecar connections, and, furthermore, reveals the owner to be a man without mechanical knowledge.

PILLION RIDING

It is now compulsory for a proper pillion seat to be used when a passenger is carried, and where a sidecar is not attached it is unlawful to carry more than one passenger. The passenger, moreover, is required to ride *astride* and not aside the machine, and must be covered by insurance. The passenger should sit still, and not lean in either direction, even when rounding corners. Although the machine itself will be "banked," or inclined, when going round a corner, the passenger should endeavour to keep his or her body in the same relation to the machine as when riding on a straight stretch of road. A pillion rider should not try to maintain the balance of the machine in traffic, or when taking corners at a low speed, by allowing his feet to touch the ground.

PROCEDURE ON HILLS

Stopping on Hills. A solo machine should always be left with the front wheel pointing *up* the hill, as in this position it cannot " lift " from its stand of its own accord. A combination should also be left in a similar manner, one of the wheels being jammed against the kerbstone or bank and the front wheel turned towards the kerb so that any movement tends to jam the wheel still harder. The low gear should also be engaged.

Starting on Hills. With regard to starting on hills, if the latter are of lesser gradient than one in seven, no difficulty should be encountered if the methods already outlined are adopted. If the hill is steeper, adopt the following procedure : Lift the clutch and apply the brake, the latter operation preventing the machine from running downhill. With the brake on, start the engine, race it a little, and with low gear engaged gradually release the brake, *at the same time gradually letting in the clutch.* This dual action requires practice in order to be carried out effectively, and the beginner may have to start his engine several times until he has acquired the knack.

Starting Downhill. Undoubtedly the best method of starting downhill is to coast down with the clutch disengaged and top gear engaged, until the machine has gathered a fair speed, when the clutch should be slowly engaged.

Braking on Hills. In descending steep hills of appreciable length when the brake would be on for some seconds, use the front and rear brakes alternately, for this prevents the parts of the brake getting very hot.

Using the Engine as a Brake. When descending very steep hills engage low gear at the *top of the hill*, and allow the machine to run down with the throttle closed. On a new machine the novice will probably be astonished at the very powerful braking action this produces. Care must be taken to open the throttle before reaching the bottom of the hill, as otherwise the machine may lose way and pull up unexpectedly.

THE HIGHWAY CODE, ETC.

The Highway Code has been issued by the Minister of Transport with the authority of Parliament under Section 45 of the Road Traffic Act, 1930. Copies of a booklet giving the Code in full are obtainable for 1d. from His Majesty's Stationery Office, Kingsway, W.C.2. The chief provisions are given below. It is important to note that whilst failure to observe provisions of the Highway Code is not an offence, for the Code has not the power of an Act of Parliament, there can be no question that such a breach would be taken into account in legal proceedings. The adoption of this Code will undoubtedly add to the safety of motor-cycling and motoring generally. The Code is intended as a supplementary guide to the proper use of the highway, and as a code of good manners to be observed by all. Those who submit themselves for the new driving tests will be examined as to their knowledge of the Highway Code.

Summary of the Highway Code. All persons have a right to use the roadway and an obligation to respect the rights of others. Keep on guard against the errors of others; never take a risk in the hope or expectation that every one else will do what is necessary to avoid the consequences of your rashness. Take special care in bad weather, for when the roads are slippery all road users have less control over their movements. Pedestrians should always walk on the footpath where one is provided; if there is no footpath it is generally better to walk on the right of the road so as to face oncoming traffic. When you intend to stop, slow down or change direction, give the appropriate signal clearly, definitely, and in good time. Recognized hand signals are illustrated in later pages of this chapter. Never overtake unless you can see sufficiently far ahead to do so with safety. Do not overtake at cross-roads. Do not cut in. When being overtaken by another driver try to help and not to hinder. Do not accelerate at such a moment. No vehicle has a right of way at cross-roads, but it is the duty of a driver on a minor road when approaching a major road to go dead slow and to give way to traffic on it. Carefully follow the indications given by the white lines. Do not leave your vehicle at a standstill in such a position as to cause an inconvenience to residents or other users of the road. Do not leave your machine standing in the highway with the headlights on. Switch over to dim. Do not leave your machine facing the wrong way at night. During daytime in foggy weather use your lights, switching on to dim. Horns should not be used unnecessarily and should not be used to show annoyance and impatience. Respect the rights of pedestrians. Aged or infirm people and young children and those in charge of them call for your especial courtesy. If the roads are wet or muddy try to avoid splashing; slow down or stop when requested to do so by those in charge of horses or other animals. Remember that as a motor-cyclist the same rules apply to you as the driver of a car. Make no attempt to gain a forward position in a traffic block by means of the narrow spaces between stationary vehicles. They may start suddenly and you will impede them and endanger yourself. Sudden noisy acceleration is disturbing and unnecessary. Pedal cyclists are instructed not to ride more than two abreast, and to get into single file when other traffic wishes to pass. They are also asked not to wobble about the road, nor to hang on to a motor vehicle for the purpose of being towed. They may not hold on to a motor vehicle even when it is stationary.

Drivers' Signals. With every driving licence is issued, by the National Safety First Association, a little booklet which should be studied, for the increased speed and volume of traffic demand that all drivers or riders of vehicles give early and intelligible warning of their intention to make any reduction of speed or change of course which may affect drivers of other vehicles, and particularly following traffic. Drivers' signals, unlike those given by the police, are simply an indication of the signaller's intention, and do not absolve their giver from first making certain that the projected manoeuvre can be carried out without unduly interfering with others. For example, signalling and turning simultaneously are practically as dangerous as not signalling at all.

Whilst superfluous hand-wagging is as exasperating as are redundant road signs, correct hand signals given distinctly, and well in advance, are an essential for safe driving. The wearing of light-coloured gauntlets, particularly at night, make signals

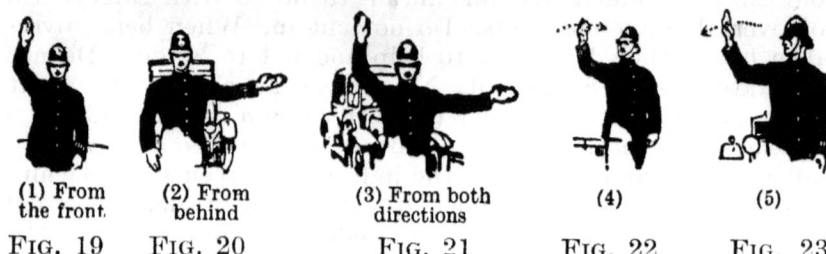

(1) From the front.   (2) From behind   (3) From both directions   (4)   (5)

FIG. 19   FIG. 20   FIG. 21   FIG. 22   FIG. 23

FIGS. 19–23. POLICE SIGNALS FOR STOPPING TRAFFIC COMING FROM THE FRONT, FROM BEHIND, OR FROM BOTH DIRECTIONS

FIGS. 22 AND 23 SIGNALS FOR RELEASING TRAFFIC

NOTE. Signals Nos. 1 and 5, or 2 and 5, are also used in combination

more visible. The three officially recommended signals are illustrated in Figs. 34 and 35. The second in Fig. 34 should be used not only before turning off to the right, but also before swerving or pulling out from the existing traffic line in order to overtake, or to avoid an obstruction. It is equivalent to a warning: " It is dangerous to overtake me on my right." If the signaller is making a complete turn to the right he should, if possible, edge over towards that side so as to leave room on his left for traffic keeping straight ahead. The three signals illustrated, judiciously used and interpreted, give all the vital indications. Until recently there were separate official recommended signals for stopping and turning left, but these have now been discarded.

Various forms of mechanically-operated direction signals are coming into use. As yet they are seldom a satisfactory substitute for the hand signal, and no standards have been officially laid down. Arrows, hands, or pointers usually give the direction, and a red or amber light, or vertical hand or arrow usually indicate " slowing down."

When approaching a traffic controller it is advisable to indicate the direction to take by the signs shown in Fig. 34.

The ordinary turning right signal gives the necessary indication and leaves no room for misunderstanding.

Police Signals. The five standard police signals are illustrated

DRIVING 49

in Figs. 19 to 23. Needless to say, implicit obedience is essential. There is only one occasion when it is permissible to proceed when the constable is holding up traffic (and even then only with his consent), and that is when turning left at a cross-road, and when traffic going straight across or turning right is being held up. If the way is clear and the constable's attention be attracted, he will usually indicate that the turn to the left may be made. Extra

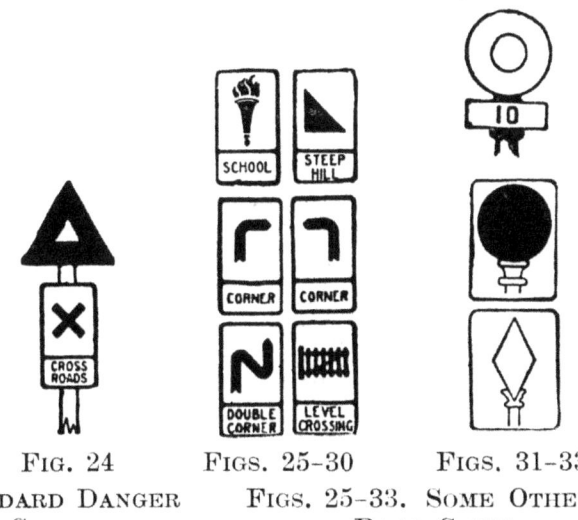

FIG. 24
STANDARD DANGER SIGNAL

FIGS. 25–30

FIGS. 31–33

FIGS. 25–33. SOME OTHER ROAD SIGNS

caution is necessary to avoid danger to pedestrians or vehicles passing across the front.

Unofficial Traffic Controllers. The signals of the uniformed patrols of the motoring organizations should be as rigidly obeyed as those of the police. Danger signals given by ordinary members of the public should be acted upon, but "all clear" signals from the same source are best ignored.

Road Signs. The familiar red triangle is the standard danger signal, and is usually combined with one of the conventional signs illustrated. In some places a ⊢ or T is used to indicate road junctions other than cross-roads. The warning signs of the responsible road users' organizations have been sited with care, but there are many unwarranted and unofficial notices (e.g. " carriage drive ") which tends to belittle the value of the genuine sign, and which, it is to be hoped, will be done away with under pending legislation. Finger-posts indicate a road junction, and are equivalent to a warning sign. Remember to look out for the 30-mile speed limit signs in built-up areas, and for automatic traffic signals. See Figs. 24 to 33.

50   BOOK OF THE B.S.A.

Other Signs. Other statutory signs are as follows: 30 M.P.H SPEED LIMIT SIGNS. Circular plate, with red outer band, black figures on a white ground, 18 in. diameter, with plate below (see Fig. 31). No speed limit area is denoted by a smaller white circle with an oblique black band. It is customary for red bands to be painted on lamp standards, tramway poles, etc., within the reduced speed limit area.

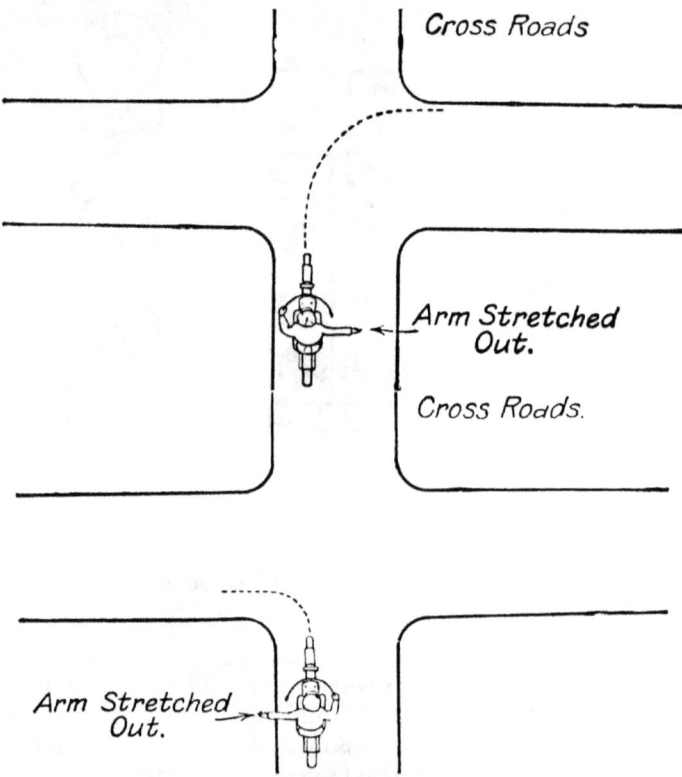

FIG. 34. HOW TO WARN FOLLOWING TRAFFIC THAT YOU ARE ABOUT TO TURN TO LEFT OR RIGHT

PROHIBITION SIGN. Circular red disc (see Fig. 32).

MOTOR NOTICE. White diamond (see Fig. 33).

PEDESTRIANS' CROSSINGS. A studded pathway across the road, denoted by a steel pillar with an amber-coloured sphere at the top.

Speed Limit in Built-up Areas. A motor-cyclist should be on the look-out for streets in which the speed limit for built-up areas applies. The Ministry of Transport definition of a built-up area is one in which lamp posts for street lighting are erected not more than 200 yards apart.

Pedestrian Crossings. A pedestrian has the right to signal traffic to stop when he desires to cross the road at a pedestrian crossing. Such are clearly marked on the road by means of steel studs, white lines, etc. Remember that it is an offence for a vehicle to stop on one of these pedestrian crossings. Pedestrian crossings are denoted by an amber coloured globe on a round steel pillar erected on the pavement adjacent.

Automatic Traffic Signals. Automatic traffic signals which are controlled by the traffic itself, consist of the red light for "stop," the amber light for "get ready" and the green light for "go." It is important to remember that a vehicle may not commence to move until the green light appears. The presence of the amber light is merely cautionary. The only exception to this rule is when, by stopping on the appearance of the amber light, you would endanger following traffic. Under these circumstances it is not an offence to proceed. In all other cases traffic in motion must immediately stop when the amber light appears. Stationary traffic as already stated, must remain stationary until the green "go" signal appears.

White Lines. White guiding lines, when suitably sited, constitute one of the greatest aids to safety on the road. When used to divide up and down traffic on sharp bends all wheels of the vehicle should, as far as possible, be kept to the left of the line. No vehicle should be parked in such fashion as to force other vehicles to cross the line.

Stop lines, running across the near side of the road, are also used to indicate the intersection of a main road—usually with " stop " or " slow " painted on the road. In towns, they are also used to hold back traffic at refuges or junctions, to leave room for pedestrians to cross.

Road Junctions. The risk of collision at road intersections is ever increasing. Contrary to common belief, no statutory authority exists giving priority to main road traffic over side road traffic, though custom imposes extra caution on traffic using the less important road.

The Proper Side of the Road. A motorist normally should keep to the left-hand side of the road, except when overtaking another vehicle, when he must pass on the off or right side.

Speed Limit. Although the general 20 miles per hour speed limit has now disappeared (the only speed limit being that of 30 m.p.h., which applies to built-up areas), a vigilant police watch on driving is kept by the mobile police force, and the motor-cyclist caught speeding may be charged with driving to the public danger.

"Dangerous driving," now heavily punished, means driving at a speed or manner *dangerous having regard to all the circumstances* actual or hypothetical, i.e. having regard to other traffic or pedestrians that are in the vicinity or might reasonably be expected to be there.

DRIVING IN TRAFFIC

Cross Roads and Corners. Cross roads and corners, perhaps, present the greatest source of danger, and one should always anticipate the presence of a badly-driven vehicle, and pass or negotiate corners at slow speed. When making a turn either to the right or to the left, adopt the scheme shown in Fig. 34, which apprises approaching as well as following traffic of your intentions. The dotted lines indicate the direction that should be taken.

How to Take a Corner. Many expert riders prefer to lean the cycle inward on a curve, and to lean the body in the opposite direction. This is probably the most satisfactory method, but it requires a little practice. The other method is to lean both the cycle and the body inwards.

Stopping in Traffic. To stop in traffic, declutch, go into neutral, and use the back brake alone, putting the latter only half on for a second or so, and then, when the machine is considerably slowed down, putting it on full.

There is no need to stop the engine as some in emergency may be tempted to do, unless the stoppage is likely to be a lengthy one. Keep the clutch disengaged and throttle the engine down until it "ticks" over. If the stoppage is of more than three or four minutes duration, it may be advisable to stop the engine to prevent it getting overheated.

As a general rule, reserve the front brake for extreme emergencies, when it should be applied at the same time as the back brake.

Warning that you are about to stop should be given as in Fig. 35, and in this respect it is important to remember that the stop should not be too sudden; you must allow the driver of the vehicle behind you time to interpret your intentions and to pull up, otherwise he may run into your back wheel or you may skid.

FIG. 35. WARNING FOLLOWING TRAFFIC THAT YOU ARE ABOUT TO STOP

Pottering in Traffic. Sometimes the reader will find that he is compelled to ride in a stream of slow-moving traffic, and he should do this by engaging low gear and closing the throttle till the engine ticks over. Or he may throttle down and use the decompressor (fitted on some older models) with second gear engaged.

Passing other Traffic. Where the width of the road allows, always pass other vehicles as widely as possible.

Led Horses. A led horse should always be led on the right-hand side of the road. It is advisable to give them as wide a berth as possible.

Passing Tramcars. Tramcars may be passed on either side, but if the offside is clear, it is wise to pass on that side, and that fact would go in one's favour in case of accident. Legally considered, the road is intended for traffic, and loitering, or travelling in such a manner as to cause an obstruction, is an offence.

Tramlines and Skids. Tramlines are dangerous at all times, but wet ones are extremely so. Therefore, if a skid is to be avoided, so should riding on the tramlines, especially if the machine is a solo. When crossing tramlines do so as near as possible at a sharp angle. There is then little danger of a skid; but to cross them at a " flat " angle is to ask for trouble.

The same instruction holds good for the stone setts of the centre rail tram system, known as the " underground " system.

Avoiding and Correcting Skids. Skidding is fairly rare if the machine is driven in the manner already outlined. Directly it is felt that the machine is getting into a skid, do not apply the brakes, as this would aggravate the trouble, but lift the clutch, and, if possible, snap the gear lever into the neutral position quickly so that the wheels are free to turn, and then, as the back wheel slides to one side, turn the bars that way, keeping the foot on the footrests, and balance will at once be regained. Get into gear again, let in the clutch and proceed.

A front wheel skid must be placed in a class by itself; it is certainly hard to correct, but it can be done if taken in time by pressing down on that side of the handlebars to which the wheel is slipping and pulling up on the other side.

Traffic Blocks. When a block of traffic can be observed some distance ahead, slow down gradually. The practice sometimes indulged in of approaching it at speed, and suddenly applying the brakes, is not altogether devoid of risk.

The Camber of the Road. Owing to the tendency of heavy vehicles to sideslip when driven on the near side of the road, the drivers of them prefer to drive on the crest. Although this may leave an equal space on either side, it is not advised to pass the vehicle on the wrong side, but to give warning of approach, so that the driver may draw in to enable his vehicle to be passed on the proper side.

Driving Behind a Tram. The short distance in which trams can pull up should be borne in mind when following one of these vehicles, and it is wise always to keep a reasonable distance behind.

Unattended Animals on the Road. Animals, such as horses, cows, pigs, sheep, etc., straying on the roadway represent a real danger, for they do the most stupid things, and when the reader may think an animal is about to leave the roadway and pass on to the grass, it will suddenly dash back into the middle of the road and make passing difficult. It is almost superfluous to tell the reader to stop in such a circumstance and to wait until the animal is well clear, or to drive it away. Do not endeavour to do this by shouting or vigorous operation of the horn; as this may cause even greater confusion.

Modifying Traffic Rules. Safety is the main consideration, and the fact that another may be in the wrong necessitates, perhaps, modifications of the rules. Dogmatically adhering to the law will not save your life when it is endangered by another breaking it, and the doctrine of " doing a great right by doing a little wrong " cannot be altogether ignored. One may thus be compelled to drive the machine on to the footpath in order to avoid a collision.

The Importance of Looking Ahead. A keen look-out ahead avoids tight corners. One may observe over the top of a hedge a horse and cart about to turn into a road on the near side. This enables one to pull up at a safe distance, and the habit of taking a sweeping survey of the view ahead is one to cultivate, and in time becomes second nature. Give ample warning of approach by sounding the horn.

NIGHT RIDING

Almost all of the remarks already given apply to night riding. A red light ahead of course signifies a vehicle either stationary or going in the same direction, and procedure is obvious.

When meeting vehicles going in the opposite direction the glare from headlamps, particularly those of cars, is a source of danger, and although many vehicles are fitted with dimming and dipping devices, this practice is not invariable.

DRIVING

Generally speaking, one should drive at slower speed at night, and a keener look-out is necessary, especially when passing through lanes adjoining fields, owing to the possibility of straying animals.

Courtesy. The great point is to be courteous on the road and considerate to others, thus fostering the friendship and brotherhood of the open road. Bearing in mind the rules given, every road user is urged to consider the safety and comfort of others.

Remember always to—

Carry your driving licence (see that it is signed) and the insurance certificate.

Keep to the left of the road.

Go slow past schools and in populous places.

Overtake on the right, after seeing that the road in front is clear.

Give warnings with the right arm when slowing down or turning to the offside.

Give way whenever possible to traffic approaching from the offside.

Conform to the lighting and registration regulations.

Recognize warning signs and speed restriction notices.

Realize the discomfort to others of dust and mud splashing.

When going down hill give way to traffic coming up.

Assist the police to regulate traffic by responding promptly to their signals.

Remember never to—

Cut in.

Overtake at cross roads, bends, in narrow village streets, or where an oncoming driver has the right of way.

Abuse the " audible warning of approach."

CHAPTER IV

HOW THE ENGINE WORKS

Elements of the Power Unit. There are three main portions of the power unit to be considered—the engine itself, the carburettor, which supplies the engine with the correct mixture of air and petrol gas, and the magneto, the duty of which is to supply a spark at the correct moment to ignite that mixture. These will now be considered.

Types of Engines. Let us deal with the engine first. There are two types into which all motor-cycle engines (and for that matter, motor-car engines) can broadly be classified—the two-stroke and the four-stroke, and in each type there are engines of one, two, or more cylinders. As, however, the number of cylinders does not affect the underlying principle (for an engine with more than one cylinder can be considered as a number of single-cylinder engines coupled together), the purpose of this chapter will be served if only single-cylinder engines are considered.

Two-stroke engines are no longer fitted to B.S.A. machines, therefore no reference will be made to the two-stroke principle.

THE FOUR-STROKE ENGINE

Elements of the Four-stroke Engine. Fig. 36 shows an ordinary single-cylinder motor-cycle engine as if it had been cut down the centre with a metal saw. It consists of the cylinder, crankcase (to which the cylinder is attached and which carries the bearings for the crankshaft), the piston, connecting rod (secured to the piston by means of the gudgeon-pin), the crankshaft (to which the connecting rod is also secured), the exhaust valve, inlet valve, induction pipe, and sparking plug. The piston is rendered gas-tight by means of piston rings. These rings are introduced to lessen the frictional area, because if the piston itself were made gas-tight in the cylinder, without any rings at all, the friction would be so great that a large amount of power would be lost in overcoming it. Connected to the induction pipe is the carburettor, which is connected by means of a pipe to the petrol tank, and driven from the crankshaft at half the speed of the latter is the magneto, which is connected by insulated wire to the sparking plug.

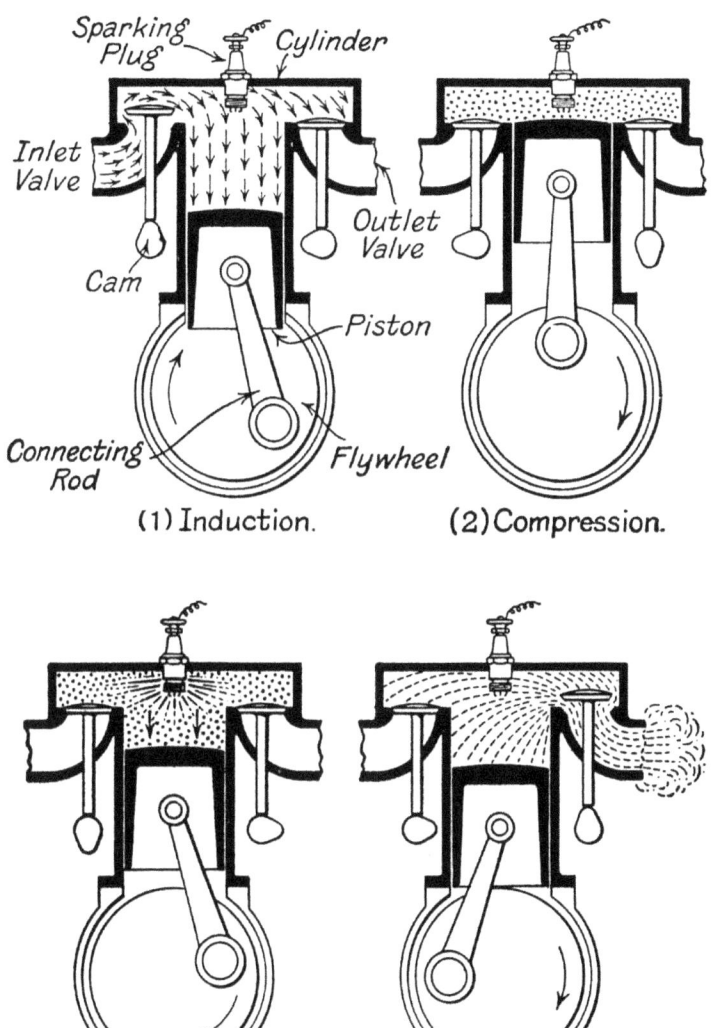

Fig. 36. The Principle of the Four-Stroke Engine

Principle of the Four-stroke Engine. It has been stated that the engine at present under consideration is known as a "four-stroke." This is because there are four distinct strokes ; firstly, the induction of the charge of petrol-and-air gas into the cylinder ; secondly, the compression of that charge ; thirdly, the explosion or ignition of it, and, fourthly, the exhausting of the burnt gases. The diagrams (Fig. 36) show the relative positions of piston and crank for these four strokes. Now, how is the charge of petrol gas introduced into the cylinder ? When the engine is caused to revolve, the piston exerts a powerful suction on the jet in the carburettor, and (1) the petrol is drawn through the induction pipe into the cylinder through the inlet valve, which is opened to allow the induced charge to pass into the cylinder by means of cams, which push on the valve stems. As soon as the piston reaches the bottom of its stroke, this valve is closed by means of the valve spring, and the piston (2), as it reverses its stroke and travels towards the top of the cylinder, compresses the charge of petrol which is trapped in it. Just before the piston reaches the top of its stroke, a spark occurs at the sparking plug point (only once every four piston strokes, be it noted) and (3) explodes the mixture, forcing the piston to the bottom of the stroke. As soon as it reaches this position, the exhaust cam operates the exhaust valve, which opens to allow the burnt charge to pass into the exhaust pipe, from whence it reaches the atmosphere after passing through the silencer.

The piston now commences to travel towards the top of the cylinder, but this time it does not compress the charge. This stroke is known as the exhaust stroke (4), because its purpose is thoroughly to scavenge the cylinder of the burnt gas. This is pushed out by the piston, and with this object in view the exhaust valve is arranged to remain open during the whole of this stroke, whilst the inlet valve remains closed. When the piston again reaches the top of its stroke, the exhaust valve closes, and the inlet valve commences to open, when the piston again sucks in a charge of petrol from the jet. And so this cycle of operations continues. It will be seen, then, how the four strokes of induction, compression, firing, and exhaust operate.

The Function of the Flywheel. Were it not for the flywheel, the piston could not possibly return to the top of its stroke, and it is the purpose of the flywheel to store up sufficient power from the power stroke to keep the engine running during the strokes of exhaust, induction, and compression.

THE MAGNETO

Its Elements. Briefly, the magneto comprises a permanent magnet with a pair of soft iron pole pieces, which form a tunnel

HOW THE ENGINE WORKS

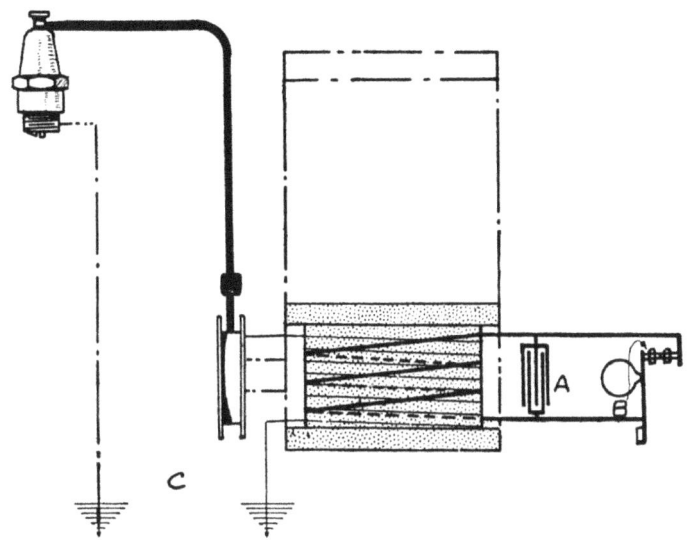

FIG. 37. CIRCUIT DIAGRAM OF MOTOR-CYCLE IGNITION SYSTEM

A. The condenser B. The contact breaker
C. The "earth" (usually the engine)

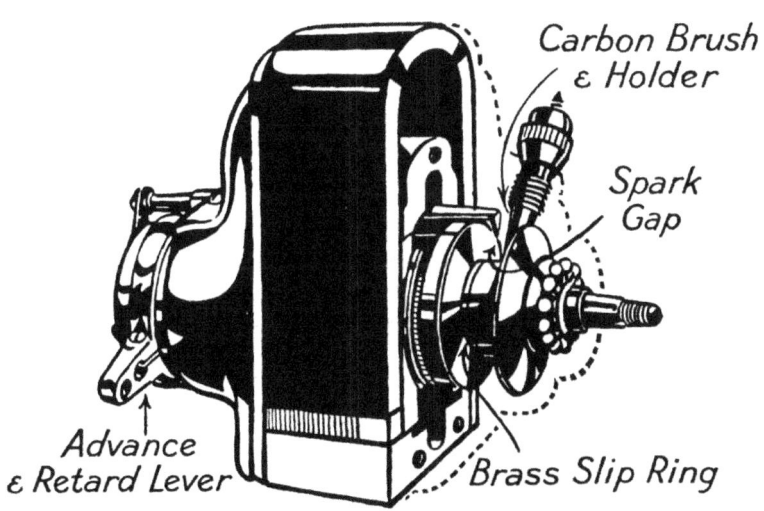

FIG. 38. THE ELEMENTS OF THE MAGNETO

which is magnetically incomplete at the top and bottom, that is, the spaces, for mechanical reasons, are merely filled with non-magnetic metal, such as brass or aluminium (see Figs. 37 and 38). In this tunnel an armature revolves, and this consists of a core built up of soft iron laminations. On this core is first wound a few layers of comparatively thick insulated wire, and the commencing end of this wire is connected to the core, or "earthed,"

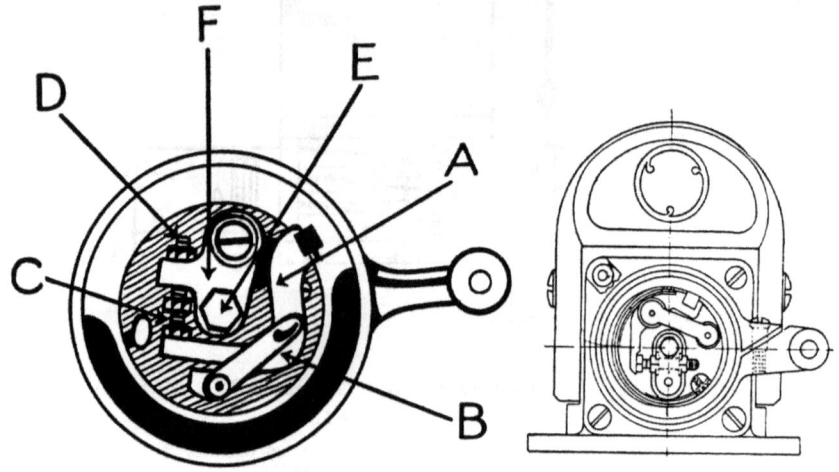

FIG. 39. TWO TYPES OF CONTACT BREAKER

A. Rocker arm *E.* Primary pin *F.* Insulated block
D. Adjustable contact point. *B.* Fibre brush *C.* Contact points

as it is termed. To the outer end of this wire is connected the beginning of another winding, which thus forms an actual continuation of the first, but in this case the wire (which is also insulated) is extremely fine—as fine as a hair, in fact—and is coiled many thousands of times round the core. As it is in this winding that the high-voltage current is generated, it is most carefully insulated from the metal parts of the machine. These two windings are called the primary and secondary, respectively. At one end of the core is mounted a condenser, which is usually enclosed in a brass case, and consists of a number of sheets of tinfoil separated by mica. Beyond this, and mounted on the end of the armature shaft, is the contact breaker.

The Contact Breaker. The contact breaker (Fig. 39) is the switch that breaks the contact, and is generally composed of a hinged steel arm, on one end of which is a platinum contact stud, and on the other end a fibre pad which rubs on a cam cut inside the contact-breaker. The platinum stud makes contact with another platinum stud fixed to a plate attached to the armature

HOW THE ENGINE WORKS

spindle. The condenser is placed in parallel with the contact-breaker to prevent sparking at the platinum points, and by so doing, conserves the electrical energy that would be wasted in feeding a useless spark. The current generated reaches its maximum intensity when the armature is at the position where its pole-faces are at the top and bottom as shown in Fig. 40. As the armature comes into this position twice per revolution, it will be seen that it should be possible to obtain two sparks per revolution, and this is done in the case of a magneto for a twin-cylinder engine. Where a single-cylinder machine is required, only one cam is fitted in the contact breaker, and thus the current is broken only once per revolution and one spark is allowed to run to waste.

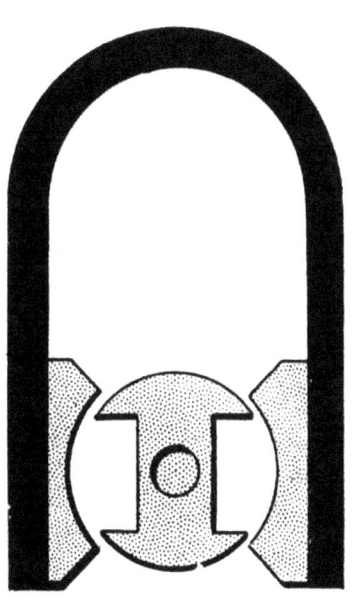

FIG. 40. THE CURRENT IS AT A MAXIMUM WHEN THE ARMATURE IS IN THE POSITION SHOWN HERE.

Single-cylinder Ignition. As the single-cylinder magneto produces one spark per revolution, and in the case of a four-stroke only one spark is needed every two revolutions of the engine, the magneto is driven at half-engine speed; while in the case of a two-stroke single-cylinder engine the magneto runs at engine speed. Twin four-stroke magnetos are also geared to run at half-engine speed, while two-stroke magnetos run at double this speed. One end of the secondary wire is attached to the primary and the other connected to a brass slip ring, against which is pressed a carbon pencil, to which is connected the wire that feeds the sparking plug.

The Armature. The armature is mounted on a pair of ball races which are lubricated when the component leaves the factory, and they therefore require but little attention. The ends of modern magnetos are provided with aluminium cover plates into which are let felt strips that assist in making the component practically watertight. On the side of the contact-breaker cover is a lever, connected by Bowden wire to a control on the handlebar. The operation of this causes the contact-breaker cover to move through a small arc of some 30°. As the cam is cut on the inside of this cover, a 30° movement allows of an alteration of timing by that amount and provides one with an advanced firing position for fast running, and a retarded one for easy starting. As, however, the further the spark is retarded the further it recedes from its maximum efficiency position, the range of advance is limited to 30°. This is one of the very few inherent disadvantages of a very reliable and useful device.

THE CARBURETTOR

Primary Functions. The primary function of a carburettor is to supply a combustible mixture to the engine. To do this the

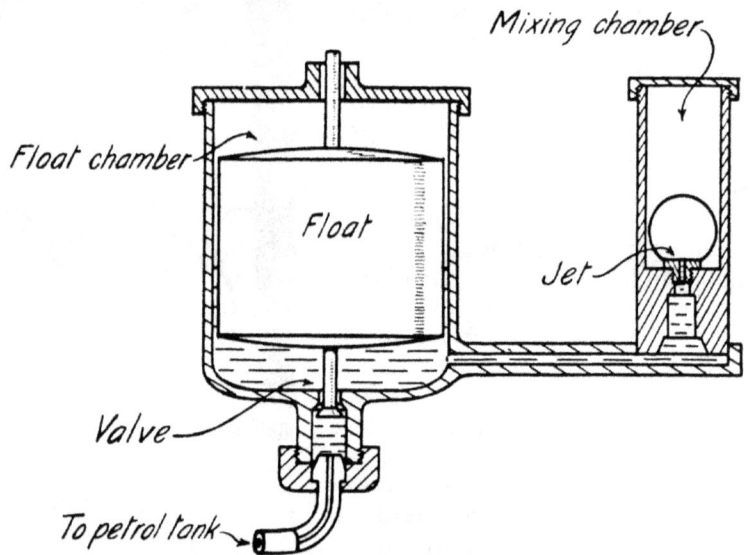

FIG. 41. DIAGRAMMATIC REPRESENTATION OF CARBURETTOR

carburettor has to measure the quantity of air passing, simultaneously measuring the corresponding amount of liquid petrol, and add the petrol to the air in the form of a fine spray, so that the petrol may vaporize readily. Figs. 41 and 42 show sections of the carburettor and its choke tube respectively.

Mixture Strength. The mixture strength should be about 14 parts, by weight, of air to 1 part of petrol for best results. An engine will run on a mixture as rich as 8 to 1, but would not develop full power, and the petrol consumption would be very heavy, as a lot of the petrol would pass out via the exhaust, incompletely burnt; on the other hand, an engine will run with a mixture as weak as 20 to 1.

HOW THE ENGINE WORKS

The Jet. To measure the minute quantity of petrol required for each power stroke by mechanical means, such as a microscopic pump, for instance, would require extremely delicate apparatus, but fortunately it can be done much more simply by means of a tiny hole, known as the jet. The size of the petrol jet is very important; a little alteration, not noticeable to the eye, will make a lot of difference in the performance of the engine.

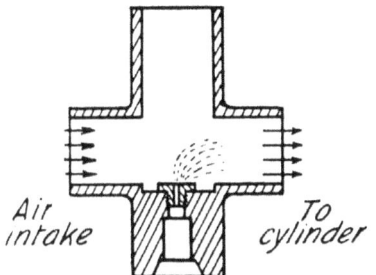

FIG. 42. DIAGRAM SHOWING HOW THE AIRFLOW "SUCKS" PETROL FROM THE JET

The Pressure Over the Jet. Besides the actual size of the jet, the pressure producing the flow has to be reckoned with. Obviously, there would be no flow of petrol through the jet unless the pressure on the surface inside the float chamber was greater than the pressure at the top of the jet. A flow could be obtained by increasing the pressure in the float chamber, but it is much easier to reduce the pressure in the region of the jet orifice by means of a venturi tube. This is generally referred to in connection with

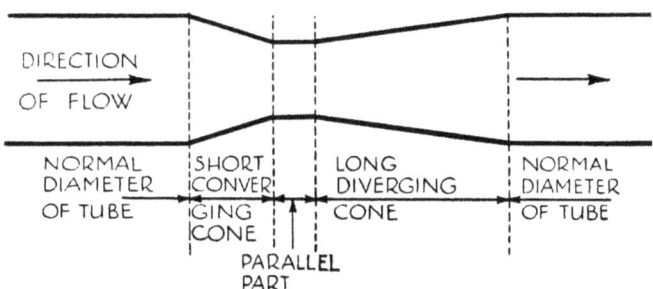

FIG. 43. THE VENTURI TUBE IS MERELY A TUBE OF THE FORM SHOWN ABOVE

carburettors as a "choke" tube. The venturi is merely a tube of varying diameter, as shown in Fig. 43.

At first the tube converges somewhat gently to a smaller diameter, then there is usually a short parallel portion of the reduced diameter, after which the tube diverges very gradually to its original diameter. It is essential that the changes in diameter should occur gradually without any abrupt changes of section to cause eddy currents.

Jet Arrangement. The jet is arranged at the throat of the venturi, where the pressure is lowest. The petrol in the float chamber being subject to full atmospheric pressure, the petrol spurts out of the jet and is broken up into a more or less fine spray. The increased air velocity by the venturi, therefore, serves the double purpose of creating a reduction of pressure, which

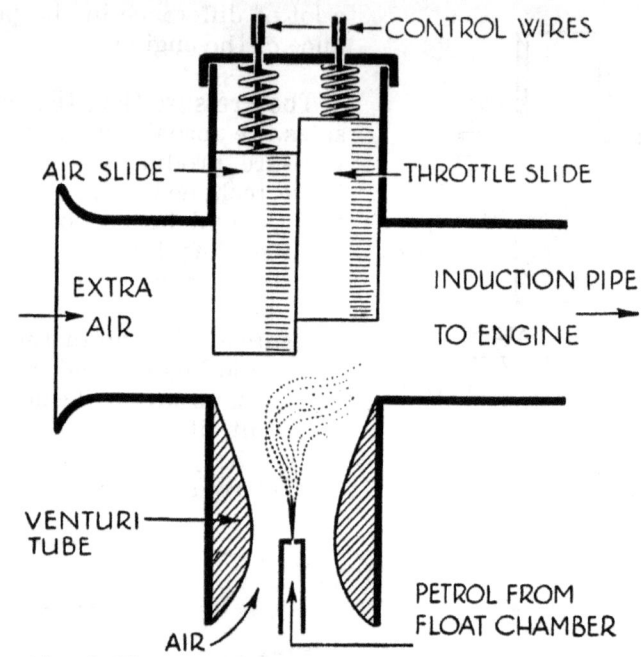

Fig. 44. A Typical Arrangement of a Venturi-type Motor-cycle Carburettor.

makes the petrol flow from the jet, and at the same time breaks up the stream of petrol into a spray.

Weakening the Mixture. A very small venturi tube is used in order to give a good suction on the jet when the throttle is nearly shut, and at full throttle, when the mixture would be too rich, it is diluted to normal strength by large quantities of extra air (see Fig. 44). This arrangement requires only one jet, and the mixture strength is adjusted by the rider to suit the conditions of the moment. He adjusts the levers to give better running; the mixture strength will not be far out if the engine runs properly.

The single-jet carburettor is, of course, easy to adjust compared with the multi-jet one, but, after the initial adjustment, the latter needs no continual " tap-twiddling " attention from the driver. Some motor-cycle carburettors have no venturi at all, while in

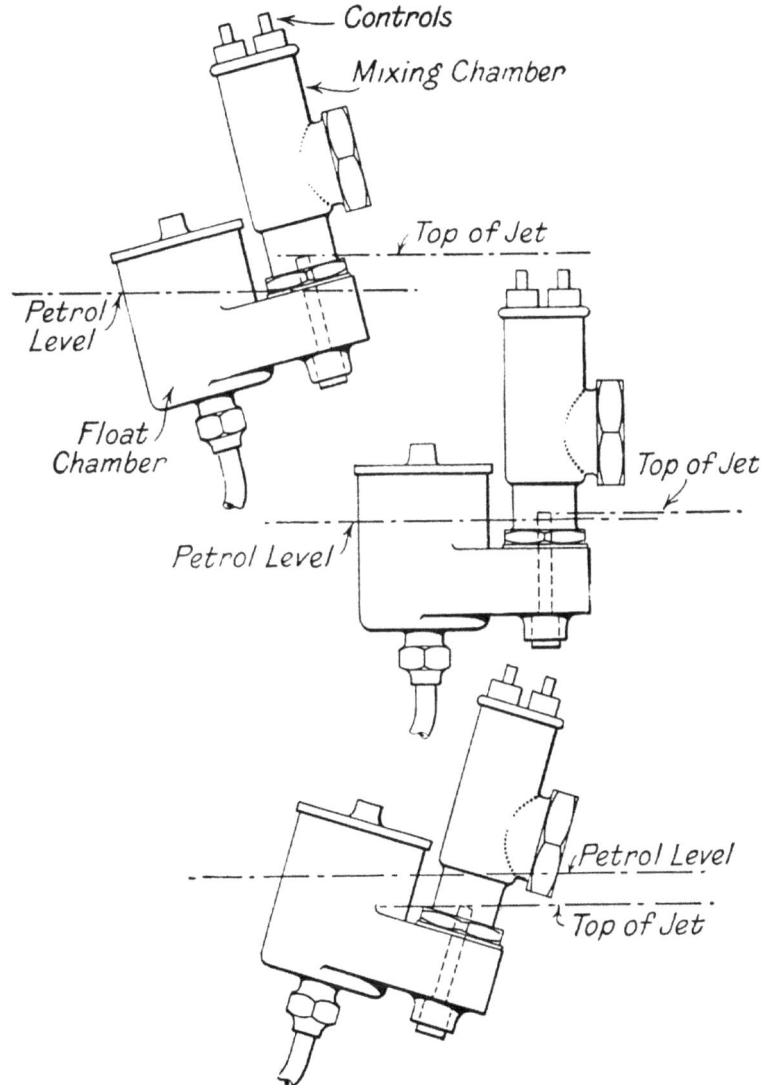

Fig. 45. Diagram showing Relation between Petrol Level and Jet, and showing how Inclining the Machine Alters the Petrol Level

some modern instruments the air intake and the induction pipe connection are formed into the shape of a venturi, with the controls at the throat providing a straight-through path for the air.

The Float and the Float Chamber. Motor-cycle carburettor float chambers are of two types—top feed and bottom feed. In the first the petrol flows from the tank to the float chamber via a pipe secured to the top of it, and in the latter the petrol enters through the bottom of the float chamber.

Inside the float chamber is a float, to which is attached a needle having a tapered end. As the petrol enters the float chamber the float, carrying the tapered needle, rises " or floats," until the tapered end of the needle closes the inlet orifice. As the engine sucks in the petrol from the float chamber via the jet, the float sinks slightly, and as the needle sinks and uncovers the petrol inlet, a fresh supply of petrol is admitted. Obviously, without a float the petrol would merely spurt out through the jet.

The Advance and Retard. The advance and retard lever is fixed to the left side of the handlebars and causes the spark to occur about $\frac{1}{4}$ in. before top dead centre in the fully advanced position, and about $\frac{1}{16}$ in. *after* top dead centre in the fully retarded position. Most engines have a " best " position for these levers, which can only be found by trial.

CHAPTER V

MECHANICAL DETAILS OF THE B.S.A.

THE beginner is usually too enthusiastic and anxious to ride his machine to bother his head about its constructional details. Sufficient for him that the machine runs. There comes the time, however, when he begins to ponder over such matters, especially when overhaul becomes necessary, or when adjustment necessitates dismantling some part of the machine. A knowledge of

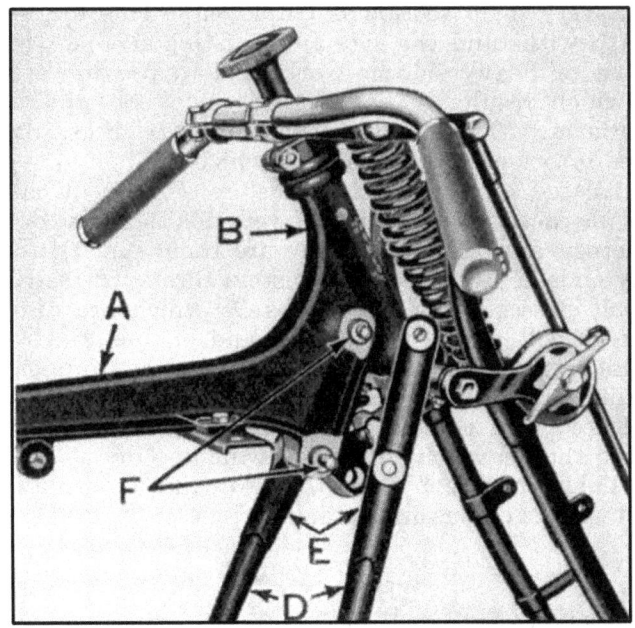

FIG. 46. THE HEAD ARRANGEMENT

the construction at such times is invaluable, for it enables him to do the particular job much more quickly than he would if he had to fumble about to find out how the various parts were secured.

When studying the machine it is easier to follow out the assembly if the parts are considered as units, and study should be directed to each unit as if the rest of the machine did not exist.

Frame. The frame of all the inclined engine models has been re-designed. The general outline and duplex cradle construction have been retained, and in its latest form it possesses immense strength without excessive weight. Instead of the tubular top member joined to the short tank rail a single high-tensile steel forging A (Figs. 46 and 47) is used, embodying the head lug B at the front end and the seat lug C at the rear, forged in one piece. The usual brazed joints at the ends and at the centre are thus eliminated, and a much stronger and more reliable construction is obtained. This gives the machine a backbone of forged steel and means greater strength, safety, and comfort.

The forging is of a wide I section which is gradually increased from rear to front in such a way that it offers uniform resistance to bending throughout its length. At the front, immediately behind the head lug, where the vertical loading on the top member is high, a very deep section is employed. This forging is also designed to withstand the side and twisting strains which occur during fast or heavy sidecar work, and to provide a degree of rigidity which results in complete stability on grease and on rough surfaces. The duplex down tubes D (Figs. 46 and 47) are brazed into separate forgings E, which are bolted to the head lug and located on substantial registers F, two of these being provided for each tube. At their lower ends the front down tubes are reinforced and trapped. They are then joined to the front chainstay ends G by means of registers through which the front engine bolt passes. The seat tubes H, which are also duplex, are securely bolted to the seat lug and engine gearbox cradle plates. Each of the chainstays extends as a continuous member to the front, where it unites with one of the front down tubes. The duplex construction of these members prevents frame distortion due to the heavy chain tension which occurs at high speeds, which is liable to absorb power and to cause transmission noise and rapid wear of chains and sprockets.

THE ENGINE

Parts of the Engine. We have already seen how the petrol engine works, and the elements of the engine (piston, crank, etc.) were explained at the time. It may, then, fairly be supposed that the reader will not require further reference to this matter.

No detailed mention has yet been made of "side-valve" engines or "overhead-valve" engines.

The Side-valve Engine. In the early forms of motor-cycles, what is known as superposed valves were used. That is to say, the inlet valve was placed immediately over the exhaust valve. The inlet valve usually was automatically operated by suction, which caused it to lift on the induction stroke and admit the

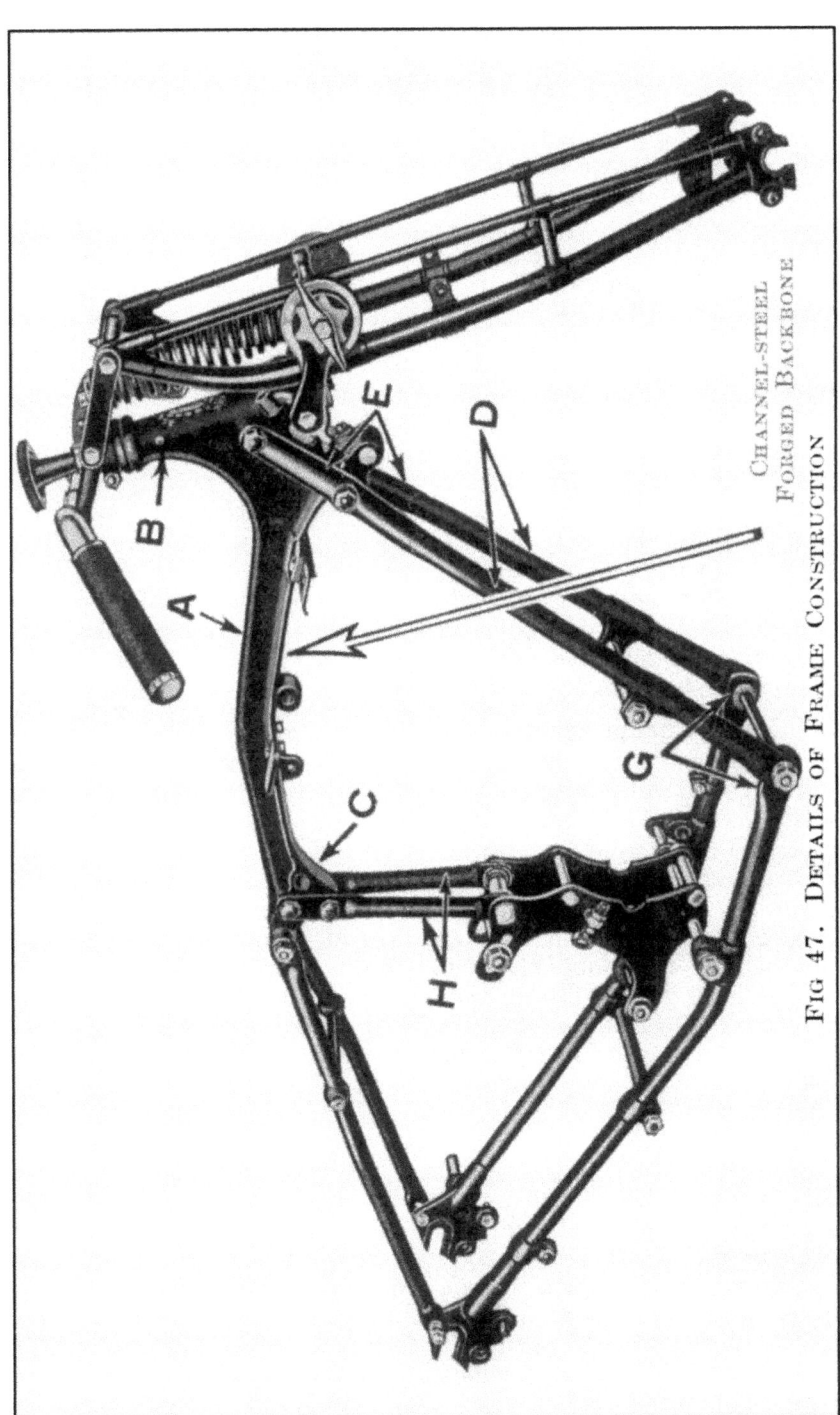

Fig 47. Details of Frame Construction

charge of petrol-and-air gas. Automatic valves, however, were so troublesome that mechanically-operated valves were introduced (the honour of introduction belongs to the Minerva Co.), and instead of the valves being superposed, they were placed side-by-side. It will be seen that the inlet valve, as well as the exhaust valve, is mechanically operated. By far the majority of cars and motor-cycles now have this valve arrangement. Mechanically-operated overhead valves are in use to-day on almost all well-known makes of motor-cycles.

The Overhead-valve Engine. Even as side-by-side valves were an improvement on superposed valves, so (theoretically, at any rate) are overhead valves an improvement on side-by-side valves. The advantages claimed for it are that a more perfect design of cylinder is possible, and that better carburation is obtainable as the turbulence (the swirling motion) of the gas, so necessary to efficient carburation, is greatly improved. Two types of overhead-valve gear are in use to-day, one carried by a detachable cylinder head, and the other in a detachable seating. An engine fitted with overhead valves is more speedy than a similar model with side valves, and, judging from present tendencies, overhead valves will be universal in a few years' time.

Inclined Engine Features. All 1935 models, except, of course, the twins, have upright engines, but the technical features apply to both. An outstanding feature of all B.S.A. motor-cycles is the generous size of all wearing parts to ensure long life with minimum attention. The alloy steel connecting rod A (Fig. 48) is scientifically designed to give strength with lightness. It transmits the surge of power to the crankpin B which is drilled with an oil passage C. A continuous current of lubricant is pumped under pressure to the double row big-end bearing D. Tapers in the forged steel flywheels grip the crankpin and the whole assembly rotates in the generous bearings. At E the mainshaft is housed in both ball and roller bearings, at F in a roller bearing (ball bearing on side valve models), and at G the oil feed is arranged. Thus, the sprocket H runs in perfect precision, giving a noiseless chain drive.

The patented design of valve gear gives up to 1,000 miles at high speed without the need to set the valve clearance. The scientific springing scheme ensures that the valve follows the cam contour up to 5,400 revolutions per minute—45 perfectly timed openings and closings a second. And all this with commendably quiet operation due to well-proportioned wearing surfaces. The timing pinion I, with wide working face, drives the cam wheels J separately. The cam wheels, on fixed shafts with central oil supply, operate circular flat base tappets L. The regular rotation

MECHANICAL DETAILS OF THE B.S.A. 71

of these presents changing contact lines to the cam action, with consequent long life.

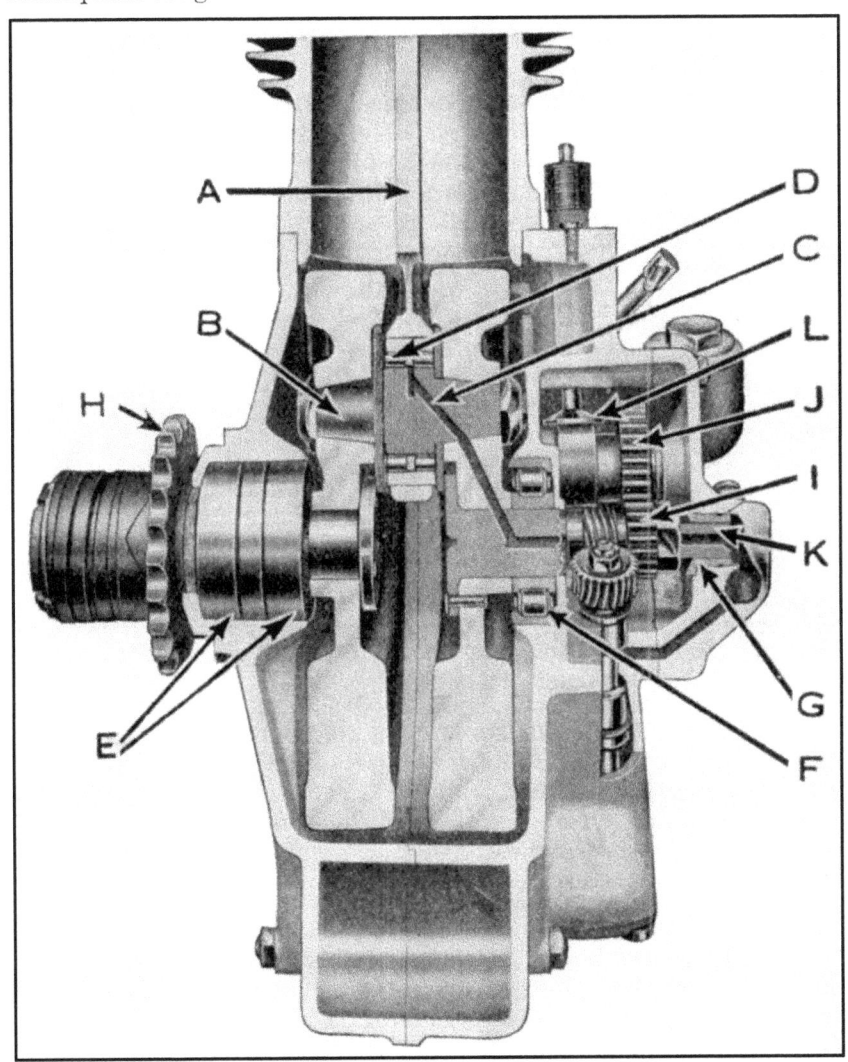

Fig. 48. Inclined Engine Features

THE CUSH DRIVE

Purpose of the Cush Drive. The purpose of a cush (short for "cushion") drive is to eliminate the harshness which accompanies the use of chain drive, and it certainly tends to reduce wear on the back tyre, and enables the power from the engine to be "picked up" gradually. With the now out-of-date belt-driven machine (or chain-and-belt) the cush drive was unnecessary, for the flexibility of the belt served the same purpose. In actual practice the friction clutch itself is a cush drive, for it slips a little when "picking up."

A cush drive of the spring-loaded cam-face type is mounted on the engine mainshaft of all the 1935 B.S.A. models. Any irregularities in the driving torque of the engine cause the driving member to recede from the sprocket against spring pressure, and so rotate slightly without driving the sprocket. This ensures an

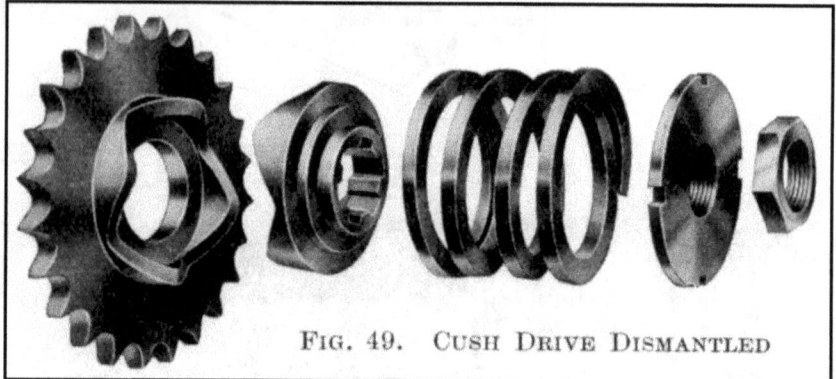

FIG. 49. CUSH DRIVE DISMANTLED

extremely smooth drive. It is automatically lubricated by oil mist from the crankcase.

New Pattern Cam-cush Drive. In the present range of B.S.A. models the cush drive somewhat resembles the ratchet mechanism of a keyless watch. In this later pattern, one large coil spring connects the engine with the countershaft, the connection between the spring mounting and the engine shaft being in the form of a cam-faced serrated plate, but capable of a little give and take on either side.

Four-Speed Gearbox. The four-speed gearbox is of the countershaft type, with all pinions in constant mesh and external clutch of the dry-plate type. Gear-changing is affected by sliding dog clutches A and B, and the method by which the dog-clutches are given the necessary movement constitutes one of the principal features of the device (see Fig. 55). On shaft C, which is rotated by the pinion, and quadrant D (Fig. 56), which is operated by a lever at side of the tank, are mounted two operating forks E and F, the arms of which engage in the grooves of the dog clutches A and B. Helical cam grooves are formed in these forks, which engage pegs G fixed in shaft C. When shaft C is revolved by means of the operating mechanisms the pegs G cause the forks

MECHANICAL DETAILS OF THE B.S.A.

E and F to slide along, the cams being cut so as to give the required position to the sliding dog clutches A and B. When first gear is put into operation dog clutch B is moved into engagement with pinion J. The drive is transmitted by means of central shaft pinion J. The drive is transmitted by means of central shaft H and pinion I to pinion J, then through dog clutch B to shaft K and pinion L, which in turn drives pinion M, to which the rear chain sprocket N is attached.

The second gear is obtained by rotating shaft C, which withdraws dog clutch B from engagement with pinion J into engagement with pinion T. The drive is then transmitted from shaft H through pinions L and T, then, as previously, through pinion L to pinion M (Fig. 59) and rear chain sprocket. Third gear is obtained in a similar manner through pinions R and S. Fourth or high gear is effected by a further movement of shaft C, which withdraws dog clutch B from pinion T and engages dog clutch A with pinion M, clutch B being retained in an inoperative position. Pinion sleeve M, with sprocket N, is thus coupled direct to shaft H, pinions J, T, R and L revolving idly. A means of ensuring correct position of all gears is arranged in the

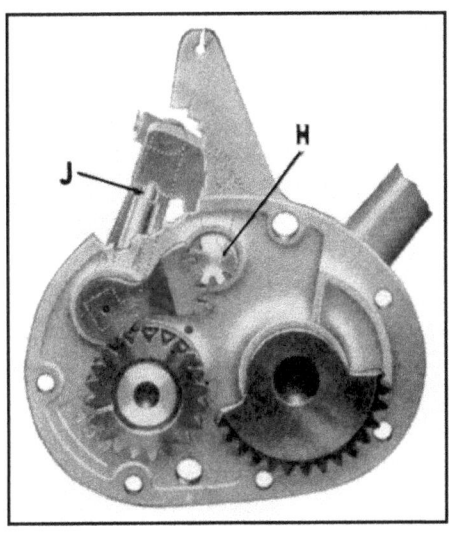

Fig. 50. Gearbox End-plate on the Light Three-speed Gearbox

gearbox operating mechanism. The quadrant D (Fig. 56) is formed with teeth round part of its circumference only. On the plain portion of the periphery a number of pockets are provided, which engage with a spring plunger mounted on boss of gearbox cover The position of the gear lever in relation to the gear is thus assured if the control rod is correctly adjusted. To start the engine the operating lever is moved to the neutral position. Each dog clutch is now out of engagement. Movement of the kick-starter crank rotates quadrant P (Fig. 58) mounted on shaft K, which in turn engages with ratchet pinion mounted on shaft H. In order that its engagement shall be certain, without jamming, the first tooth in quadrant P is of special form. All difficulty of engagement is thus obviated. On the road the engine can only be started by means of the kick-starter with the gear in "neutral" position.

Three-speed Gear (1·49 h.p. O.H.V., 2·49 h.p. S.V., and 2·49 O.H.V.). The drive on top gear is effected by sliding pinion A so that its dog teeth engage with those on pinion B (see Fig. 56).

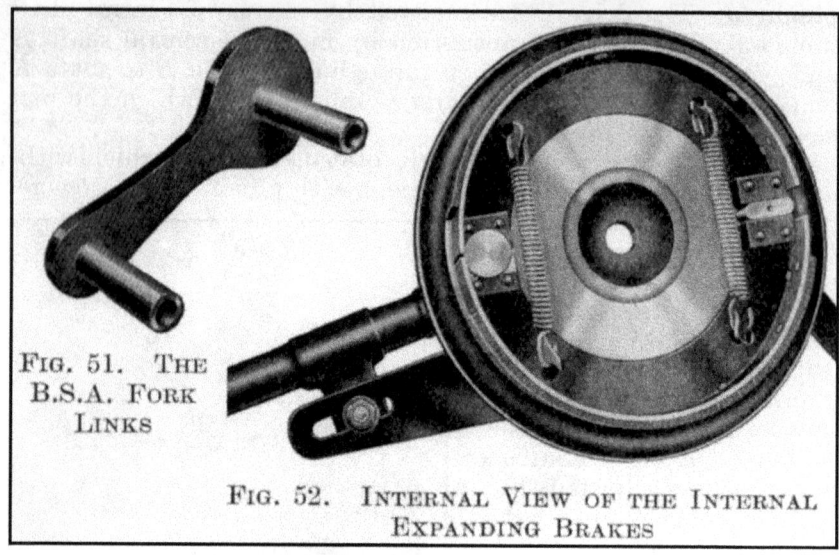

Fig. 51. The B.S.A. Fork Links

Fig. 52. Internal View of the Internal Expanding Brakes

Fig. 53. The Aluminium Piston
Note the Gudgeon-Pin Fixing
There are now no oil grooves in the skirt

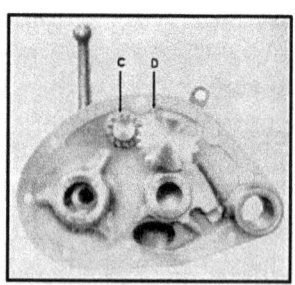

Fig. 54. End-plate of Three-speed Gearbox Fitted to the 9·86 h.p. Model

The middle gear is obtained by first withdrawing pinion A from engagement with pinion B and then sliding pinion C so that its dog teeth engage with fixed pinion D. Low gear is obtained by disengaging pinion C from pinion D, then sliding pinion A into

MECHANICAL DETAILS OF THE B.S.A.   75

engagement with loose pinion E. The necessary axial movement of the gears A and C on their shafts is obtained by means of the operating forks F and G respectively, which engage in grooves in the gears. Pegs on the control shaft H working in helical cam slots in the forks convert the rotary movement of the outside gear lever (through a quadrant and gear) into the sliding motion of the operating forks. A spring-controlled plunger on the gear control lever registering in depression in the control plate gives definite location to the gears.

The Three-speed Countershaft Gear fitted to the 9·86 h.p. Model G.35-14. This three-speed gearbox is of the countershaft type, with all pinions in constant mesh, and an external clutch of the dry-plate variety.

The Dog Clutch. The changing of gears is effected by sliding dog clutches A and B (Fig. 59), and the method by which the dog clutches are given the necessary movement constitutes one of the principal features of the device. (See also Figs. 54, 57, and 58.)

On the shaft C (Fig. 59), which is rotated by means of the pinion and quadrant D, which is operated by the lever at the side of the tank, are mounted two operating forks E and F, the arms of which engage in the grooves of the dog clutches A and B. Helical cam grooves are formed in these forks, which engage pegs G fixed in shaft C. When the shaft C is revolved by means of the operating mechanism, the pegs G cause the forks E and F to slide along, the cams being cut so as to give the required position to the sliding dog clutches, A and B.

The Low Gear. When the low gear is put into operation, the dog clutch B is moved into engagement with pinion J. The drive is transmitted by means of central shaft H and pinion I to pinion J, then through dog clutch B to shaft K and pinion L, which in turn drives pinion M, to which the rear chain sprocket N is attached.

The Second Gear. The second gear is obtained by rotating shaft C, which withdraws dog clutch B from engagement with pinion J into engagement with pinion T. The drive is then transmitted from shaft H through pinions O and T, then, as previously, through pinion L to pinion M and rear chain sprocket.

The High Gear. The high or normal gear is effected by a further rotating of shaft C, which withdraws dog clutch B from pinion T, and engages dog clutch A with pinion M, clutch B being retained in an inoperative position. Pinion sleeve M, with sprocket N, is thus coupled direct to shaft H, pinions

76 BOOK OF THE B.S.A.

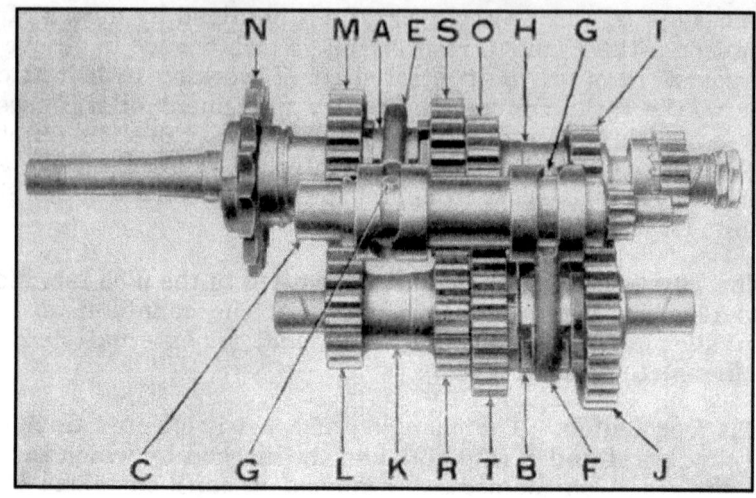

Fig. 55. Internal View of the Four-speed Gear

Fig. 56. Arrangement of the Gears on the Light Three-speed Gearbox

MECHANICAL DETAILS OF THE B.S.A.

J, T, and L revolving idly. When changing up from low to high gear it is imperative that the drive of the engine should be disengaged momentarily by releasing the clutch.

Engagement of Dog Clutches. A novel means of ensuring correct position of all gears is arranged in the gearbox operating mechanism. The quadrant D is formed with teeth round part of its circumference only. On the plain portion of the periphery a number of pockets are provided, which engage with a spring plunger mounted on the boss of the gearbox cover. The spring plunger on change lever is thus dispensed with.

Starting the Engine. To start the engine, the gear lever is moved to the neutral position. Each dog clutch is now out of engagement. Movement of the kick-starter crank rotates quadrant P mounted on shaft K, which in turn engages with ratchet pinion mounted on shaft H.

Foot-operated Gear Change. The following description (see Fig. 60) of the B.S.A. foot-operated positive gear-change is given with the object of enabling the rider more easily to dismantle and re-assemble the device in the event of such operations ever becoming necessary. The pedal A is adjustably coupled to the operating plate B, which is free to rotate on the fixed shaft C. When pedal A is depressed, therefore, the plate B is caused to rotate through an angle. During the initial part of its travel it bears on the extension D on pawl E, thus forcing the latter into engagement with a tooth in the ratchet plate F, which is extended at G to form a lever connected to the gearbox operating shaft. During the remainder of the pedal stroke the pawl is firmly meshed with the ratchet plate and it therefore carries it bodily round with it. The travel of the operating plate, and, with it, of the pedal, is limited by an abutment J on the stop plate G, with which a similar abutment K on this plate comes into contact. While pawl E is in operation as just described, pawl L is kept clear of the ratchet by spring M. It will be seen from the above that the downward movement of the pedal moves the lever G on the ratchet plate to the right one step. On being released the pedal returns to its original position under the action of spring N and the pawl E slips back over the tooth on the rachet plate and remains in readiness to engage with the next tooth should a further depression of the pedal be made. The downward movement of the pedal causes a change to a higher gear. To change down to a lower gear the pedal is raised from its central position, and the action is exactly similar, except that pawl L is in operation while pawl E remains clear of the ratchet plate. The spring-loaded

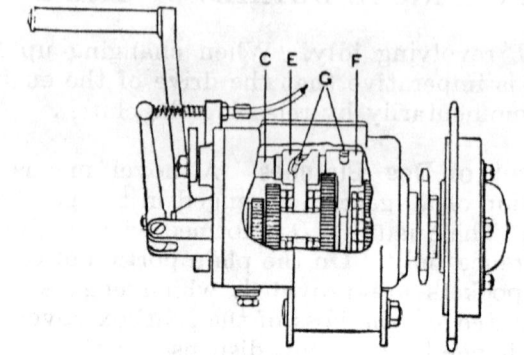

Fig. 57. Three-speed Gearbox
(Outside View)

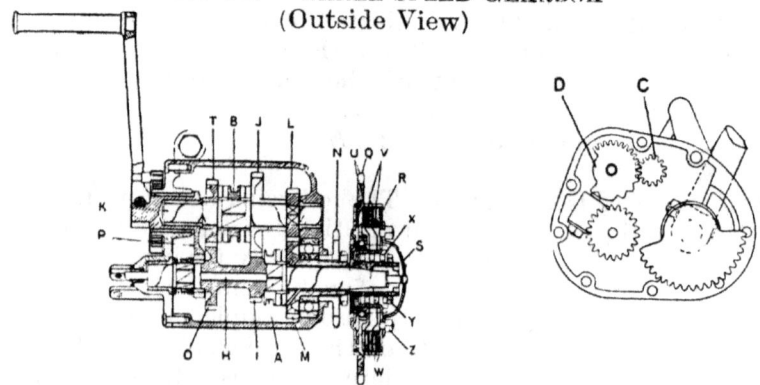

Fig. 58. Three-speed Gearbox (Inside View)

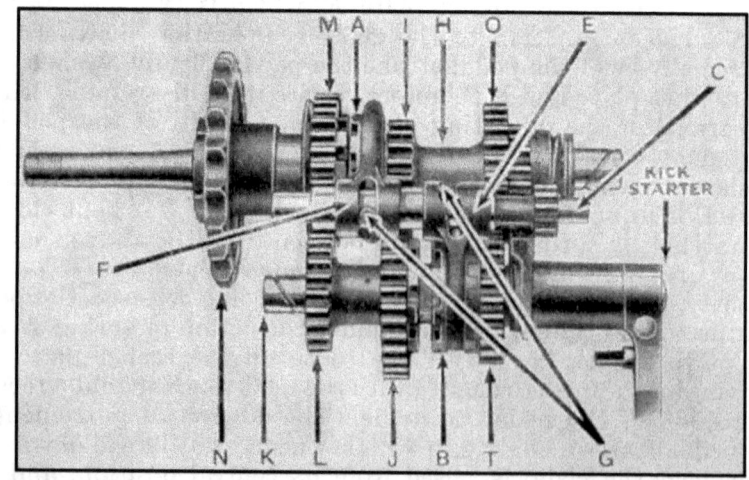

Fig. 59. An Internal View of the Gearbox, with the Clutch Removed

MECHANICAL DETAILS OF THE B.S.A.

plunger *O* acts as a positive locating medium for the pedal in the central position.

Neutral position is obtained between first and second gears by depressing the pedal a half-stroke from the first gear position or by raising the pedal a half-stroke from second gear. The possibility of the gear slipping out of neutral is prevented by the spring-loaded plunger in the gearbox.

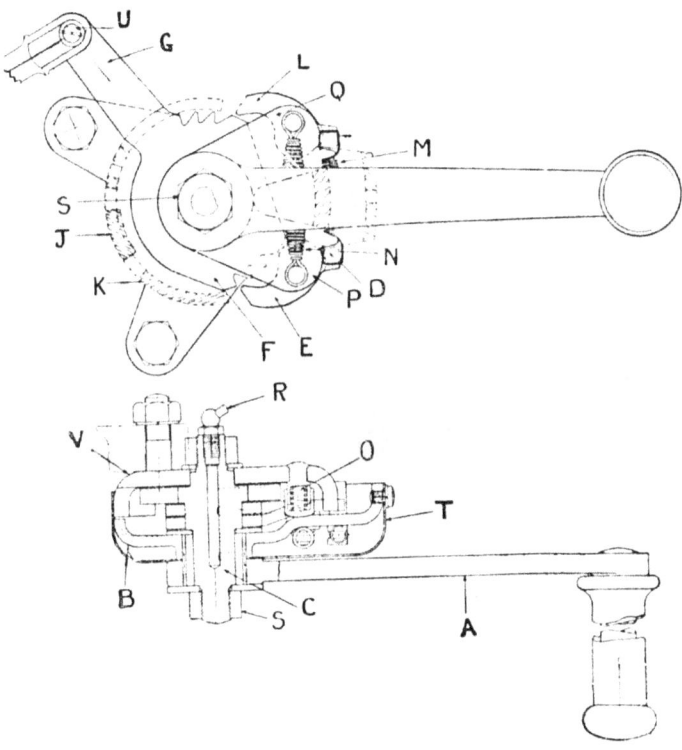

FIG. 60. SHOWING THE ACTION OF THE FOOT-OPERATED GEAR CHANGE

Lubrication of Foot Gear Change. The moving parts of the B.S.A. foot gear change, which rotate on the fixed shaft *C*, are the operating plate *B*, the pawl arms *P* and *Q*, and the ratchet plate *F*. These are lubricated through oil holes in the shaft from nipple *R*. For this purpose it is advisable to use engine oil in preference to grease. This can be applied in the usual way by means of the grease gun. Lubricate in this way every 500 miles. The other moving parts—the pawls *E* and *L*—should be lubricated every 500 miles (or more frequently if it is found necessary) by means of an oilcan.

Dismantling and Reassembling. In the ordinary course of events the only attention, apart from lubrication, that the gear change is likely to require is the replacement of a broken spring. For this reason it is advisable to carry a set of spare springs, M and N. To replace them in the event of breakage (which is, however, a very rare occurrence) it is necessary to remove nut S, take off the large washer behind it, and replace the nut; this will hold the mechanism together while removing the pedal. Draw off pedal A, using if necessary the small screw from the rear of the cover, in the tapped hole normally concealed by the washer, as a fulcrum (this is not shown in the illustration), undo the other spring holding

Fig. 61. The B.S.A. Clutch Dismantled

cover T in position, when the springs will be exposed. Remove the broken spring and fix the new spring by pressing its eyes over the anchoring lugs. This can be done conveniently with a pair of pliers.

To dismantle the mechanism completely it is only necessary, having taken off the pedal, cover, and springs as described above, to remove the screw U and withdraw the remaining parts from the fixed shaft, rocking them slightly the while to prevent jamming and taking care not to lose the plunger and spring O. The parts should be carefully examined and any showing signs of undue wear should be replaced by new ones. Thoroughly clean and smear the parts with oil before reassembling. Having made certain that everything is in order, first replace the ratchet plate F, then each of the pawl arms in turn. Note that these are not interchangeable, and that the obvious order of assembly is that which brings the pawls into line with the ratchet plates. Next, place the spring loaded plunger *O* in its socket, and slide the operating plate over the shaft. There may be a little difficulty in getting the operating plate to slide right home, but careful manipulation of the pawls and pawl arms will facilitate this. Replace the springs *M* and *N*, and finally refit the cover pedal, washer and nut.

THE CLUTCH

The Clutch. This is of the floating dry-plate type. On the larger models it consists of seven friction rings and eight steel

FIG. 62. THE B.S.A. PLATE CLUTCH

plates arranged alternately. There are thus fourteen bearing surfaces with a total area of more than 200 sq. in.—an unusually large area for a motor-cycle clutch (Figs. 61 and 62). Every second steel plate is coupled by splines to the clutch drive which is driven by the primary chain. The other steel plates are splined to the clutch sleeve which is keyed on to the gearbox mainshaft. There are six clutch springs, and when the clutch is engaged these force the steel plates and friction rings together in such a way that the entire assembly rotates as a solid mass transmitting power from the engine shaft to the gearbox mainshaft. The large bearing area and effective diameter of the plates permit the use of medium strength springs. The clutch is, therefore, light to handle and sweet in engagement, and it possesses that delicacy of control which contributes so largely to the pleasure of driving. In the smaller models a lighter clutch of similar construction is fitted.

The clutch is provided to enable the driver to " disconnect " the drive from the gearbox to the rear wheel when desired, and to enable the power from the engine to be gradually taken up. The half-tone (Fig. 61) in conjunction with the details given in the paragraph on the countershaft gear, makes further explanation unnecessary.

Note the order in which the plates *U*, *V* and *W* are arranged, so that they can be assembled in the same order. (See Figs. 57 and 58.)

GENERAL LUBRICATION SYSTEM APPLICABLE TO MOST MODELS

Sump Lubrication on Inclined Engine Models. (Also applies to 1935 models.) The lubrication system of all the inclined engine models is designed on car lubrication principles, and is a vast improvement over the old type of mechanical oil pump. It cuts out all external oil pipes, which are liable to break or become stopped up, and ensures greater efficiency in the lubrication of the most vital part of the engine—the big-end bearings. The big-end bearings of B.S.A. models equipped with a circulating sump lubrication system receive 250 times as much oil as the big-ends in engines fitted with the ordinary system, yet the oil consumption is remarkably economical.

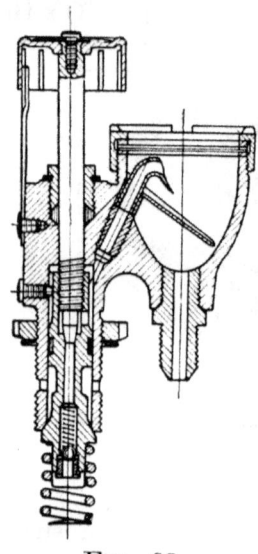

FIG. 63
CROSS-SECTION OF THE SIGHT-FEED AS FITTED TO SOME PRE-1933 MODELS

The oil is contained in the double sump *A* (Fig. 64), passes through the reservoir *B*, and past the adjustment valve control *C* to the pump *D*. It is then driven up the passage *E* into the tell-tale chamber *F*, forces out the tell-tale plunger, enters the hollow crankshaft *G*, and so through holes drilled in the flywheel and crankshaft to the big-end bearing. After cooling and lubricating this bearing, the oil is thrown on to the cylinder walls and the underside of the piston. It returns to the crankcase and is picked up and carried round by the flywheels. The scraper *H* returns it to the sump. The pump is driven by worm gear *J* from the main shaft, and being submerged, is always full of oil and cannot fail to operate. Once the correct setting for the control knob is obtained you need never touch it again. So long as you replenish the sump every few hundred miles the pump will faithfully provide perfect lubrication. See also a later page for details of the lubrication systems of the twin-cylinder models.

Sump Lubrication on Lightweight Models. On all of the lightweight models the lubricating system is similar in principle to the sump lubrication on the inclined engine models, differing only

MECHANICAL DETAILS OF THE B.S.A. 83

in detail. The oil is contained in the sump A (Fig. 64), passes through the filter B, up the hole C to the pump, forcing out the tell-tale plunger on its way. The pump delivers oil past the adjustable control valve, and through the hollow mainshaft and drilled holes in the flywheel and crankpin to the big-end bearing.

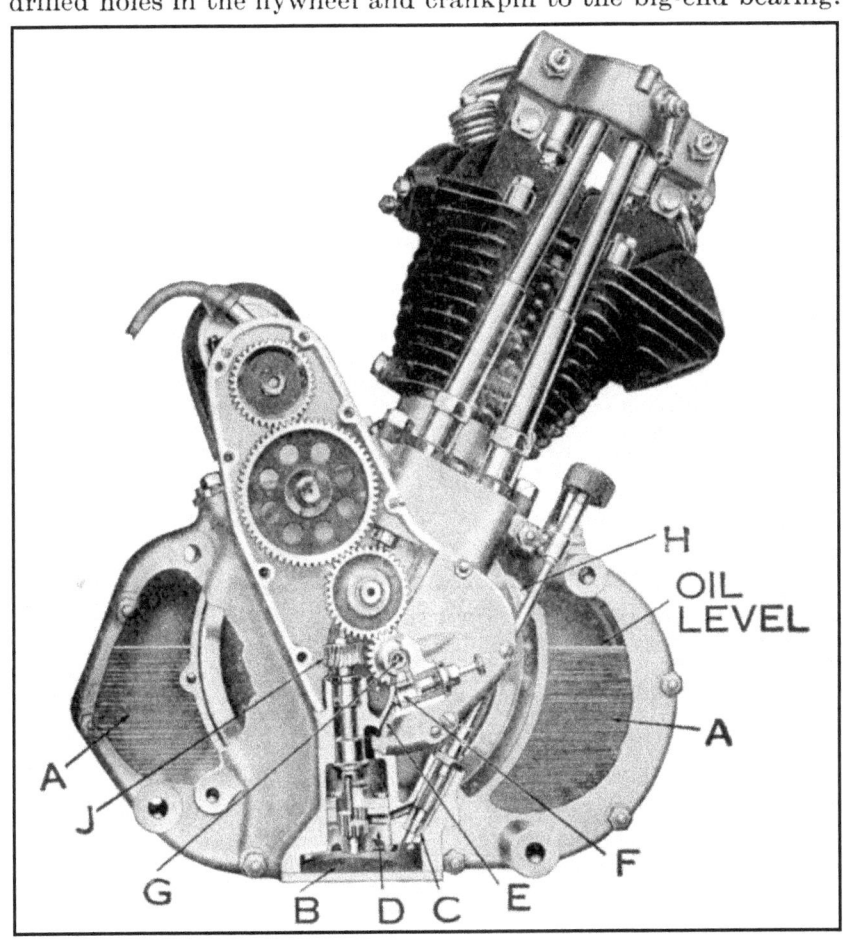

FIG. 64. THE OIL SUMP IN DETAIL

A portion of the oil is diverted to the timing and mainshaft bearing. After cooling and lubricating this bearing the oil is thrown on to the cylinder walls and the underside of the piston. It returns to the crankcase and is picked up and carried round by the flywheels. The scraper D returns it to the sump. An automatic release valve between the pump and control valve regulates the oil pressure in accordance with the control valve setting. Once the correct setting for the control knob is obtained

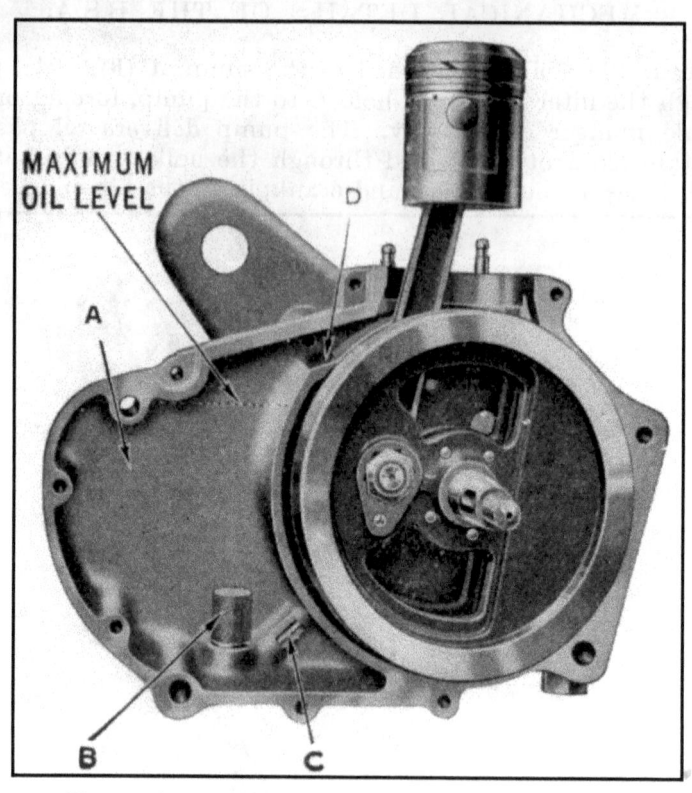

Fig. 65. View of the 2·49 h.p. Oil Sump

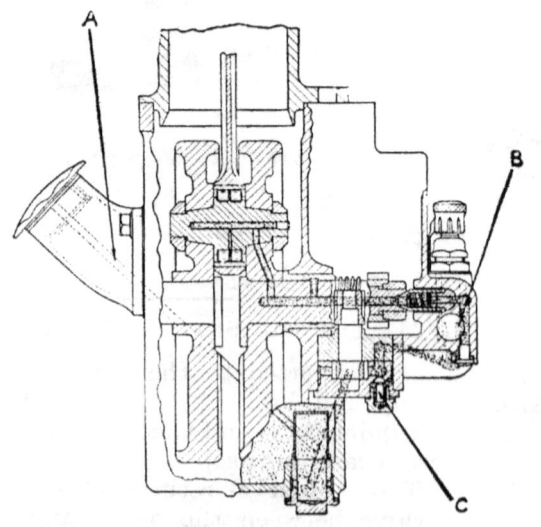

Fig. 66. Section showing Oil-feed in Big-end (Dry Sump Lubrication System)

you need not touch it again. So long as you replenish the sump every few hundred miles the pump will faithfully provide perfect lubrication.

The Lubricating System Described in Detail. Cast integral with the crankcase is a sump the capacity of which is $2\frac{1}{2}$ pints. The gear-type pump, driven by skew-gearing from the timing-side mainshaft, rotates at one-sixth engine speed and delivers filtered oil to the big-end bearing through passages cut in the crankcase, timing-cover, mainshaft, flywheel, and crankpin. The oil enters

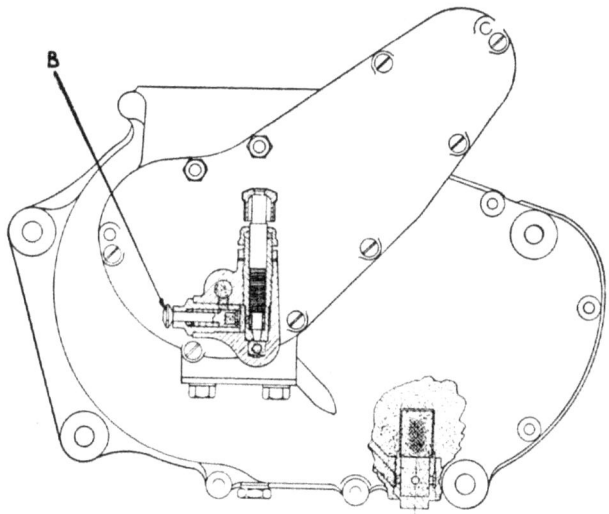

FIG. 67. DRY SUMP LUBRICATION SYSTEM

the annular space between the two rows of rollers and the centre portion of the phosphor-bronze cage. A portion of the oil from the pump is pressure-fed to the timing-side mainshaft bearing (see Fig. 67).

After lubricating the big-end the oil reaches the other parts of the engine by splash. Any excess of oil is picked up by the flywheel rims from the bottom of the crankcase and is removed by a scraper acting on the flywheels and returned to the sump. The oil supply is controlled by a valve on the delivery side of the pump. The valve is easily accessible to the rider from the saddle.

On the intake side of the pump a tell-tale is fitted. This takes the form of a small spring plunger (B, Fig. 67), which is forced outwards by the passage of oil mounted on the timing-cover and visible from the saddle. So long, therefore, as the pump is working the tell-tale projects. An automatic release valve (C, Fig. 66) is arranged between the pump and the control valve. This regulates the oil pressure in accordance with the control valve setting.

An oil level dipper-gauge (*A*, Fig. 66) is attached to the sump filler cap. This consists of a rod which projects within the sump, reaching to the bottom. The rod is of D-section, and on the flat side pint graduations are marked. To test the oil level in the sump it is only necessary to remove the dipper by unscrewing the sump filler cap and examining it. If the oil level on the dipper-gauge is indistinct, wipe it clean, reinsert, and withdraw it again. It will then be very clearly marked. The filler is mounted at the side of the sump in such a position that oil can be filled up to the correct level but not above it. It is provided with a cap which can be tightened by hand without the use of a spanner.

Lubrication is arranged for the engine shaft cush-drive by oil mist passing from the crankcase through a hole in the mainshaft. A special oiling device for the front chain consists of a small reservoir formed on the inner near-side crankcase wall. Oil accumulates in this and passes through an adjustable valve, accessible to the rider, and thence through a special hollow stud placed so that oil emerging from it drips on to the front chain.

Instructions for Lubrication. For ordinary running the oil pump control valve should be opened (turned to the left) from half to three-quarters of a turn. This setting is only arbitrary, and the rider should find out for himself the most economical setting consistent with adequate lubrication. The tell-tale provides the best guide for correct oil control setting. If it projects about $\frac{1}{4}$ in. the setting is about correct. If it moves out farther than this the setting should be reduced. If the tell-tale moves in and out continuously instead of remaining stationary, it is a sign that the engine is not receiving sufficient oil due to the control not being far enough open or to the sump becoming empty. These instructions apply for normal touring speeds. If the machine is consistently driven at high speeds the setting should be increased slightly. When the engine is new the oil supply should be fairly generous for the first 500 miles. The engine should be given about 25 per cent more oil than the above settings indicate.

Attention should be paid to the following points in connection with the lubricating systems: Check the oil level in the sump regularly by means of the dipper (*A*, Fig. 66). When the level falls to the notch marked " $\frac{1}{2}$ " the sump should be filled up with $\frac{1}{2}$ pint of oil. If preferred, the sump can be filled up with $1\frac{1}{2}$ pints of oil when the level falls to the mark " $1\frac{1}{2}$ " on the dipper. It is of the utmost importance, however, not to run more than

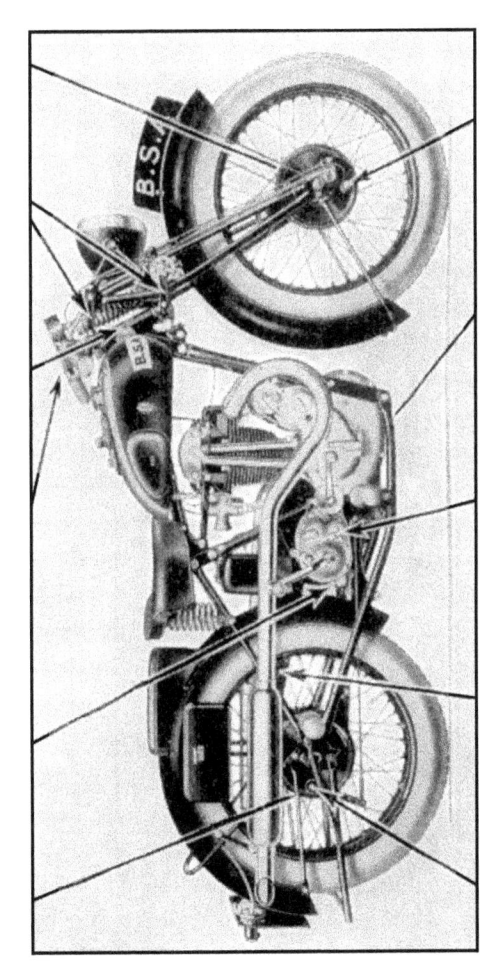

FIG. 68. LUBRICATING DIAGRAM FOR B.S.A. 2·49 H.P. O.H.V., 3·48 H.P. O.H.V., AND 4·99 H.P. O.H.V. MOTOR-CYCLES

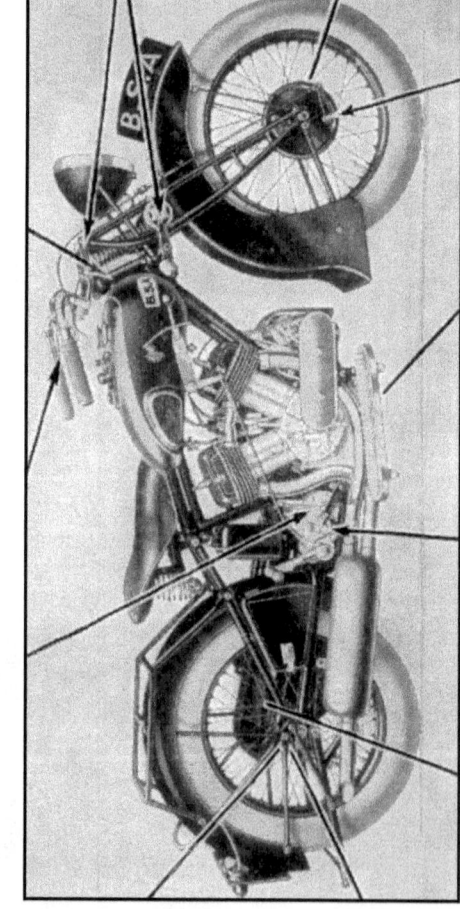

Fig. 69. Lubrication Diagram for B.S.A. 9·86 h.p. Twin Motor-cycles

MECHANICAL DETAILS OF THE B.S.A. 89

about 20 miles after the oil level has fallen to the mark "$1\frac{1}{2}$." If this distance is exceeded engine trouble may occur due to lack of lubrication.

When the engine stops firing the tell-tale should be gradually drawn in under spring pressure. If it remains out this may be due to the presence of grit or dust on the stem, and the latter should be cleaned with a piece of rag. If a very heavy oil is used it may be necessary to push the tell-tale home with the fingers.

FIG. 70. THE CAMS FOR RAPID CHAIN ADJUSTMENT
The alignment of the wheel is automatic

THE FRONT FORKS

Fig. 51 shows the type of spring fork link fitted to the B.S.A. models. These forks, it is hardly necessary to state, are for purposes of absorbing road shocks, and insulating the rider from the vibration caused.

An important feature of B.S.A. forks is the design of the links. Long spigots formed on the links enter the fork yokes and take the entire load on the forks. A greater bearing area is thus provided, and wear on the link mechanism is considerably reduced. The space between the ends of the spigots acts as a reservoir for lubricant.

HANDLEBAR FITTING

Reversible handlebars are fitted to some of the 1935 B.S.A. motor-cycles. The upturned position is suitable for touring or when the machine is used with a sidecar. When fitted downturned a sporting position is obtained.

The bars are adjustable to give a choice of wrist angle in both positions. Long rubber grips are fitted to the bars.

Fig. 71. The B.S.A. Timing Gear

THE TIMING GEAR

It will have been gathered from the previous chapter that the inlet valve must remain open for about half a revolution of the crank, and the exhaust for a further half revolution. It is the purpose of the timing gear to ensure this, and a cam (see Fig. 71) lifts the inlet valve by means of an adjustable tappet, at the commencement of the suction stroke, and permits it to close at the bottom of the stroke. It operates once for every four strokes of the piston. The exhaust valve is similarly operated, commencing to open at about the end of the power stroke. The 2·49 h.p. model has a gear-driven magneto, thus dispensing with the magneto driving chain.

The Hinged Rear Mudguard and Rear Stand. On the 3·48 h.p. O.H.V. and larger models, the new design of rear mudguard,

FIG. 72. THE HINGED REAR MUDGUARD

which is used in conjunction with a low-lift spring-up rear stand, reduces very considerably the amount of exertion required when the rear wheel is removed for any purpose. When the machine is on the stand the rear wheel is only raised about 3 in. from the ground. It is obvious, therefore, that the effort required to raise the machine on to the stand is small. By undoing two nuts at the ends of the lower mudguard stays the hinged portion is released, and it may be swung up as shown in the illustration. The rear wheel may then be drawn clear of the machine with ease.

Hubs and Brakes. The use of taper rollers for the wheel bearings ensures that heavy loads may be carried over rough roads for prolonged periods with the minimum of wear. Adjustment is easily carried out, but owing to the substantial nature of the bearings, it is only necessary at long intervals. The large diameter high-grade steel spindle is of ample strength to withstand the most strenuous conditions. The brakes are of the internal expanding type. The brake shoes are steel pressings, light, and yet sufficiently strong to resist heavy stresses without distortion. The generous width of the linings gives a large contact area, so that a powerful retarding effect is obtained with

Fig. 73. The Hub Construction

medium brake shoe pressure. A large range of adjustment is provided for the shoes. The brake cover plate is specially formed to extend over the brake drum to render the whole weatherproof. Grease and oil from the wheel bearings are excluded from the linings by means of pen steel and felt washers. The quickly detachable front hub fitted to the 9·86 h.p. G33-13 model is slightly different in construction, but embodies all the above features.

Shock Absorbers. The advantages of properly designed shock absorbers are many. Instead of having a strong spring with a harsh rebound, the modern spring fork is fitted with a comparatively light and resilient spring, the action of which is controlled

MECHANICAL DETAILS OF THE B.S.A. 93

by the shock absorbers in such a way that the machine floats over rough surfaces without violent deflection and rapid rebound.

The B.S.A. shock absorbers consist of two steel discs A (Fig. 74) with a friction disc between them. One of the steel discs is fixed to the forks and the other to the fork link. The three discs are pressed together by means of a star spring B. When the forks deflect, the rate of movement of the links is governed by the

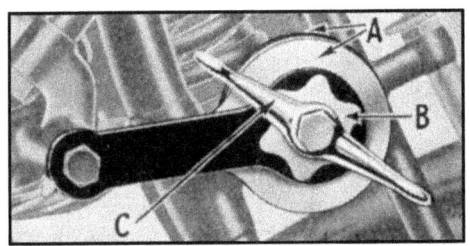

FIG. 74. THE SHOCK ABSORBERS

pressure of the star spring, and this in turn is controlled by the quickly adjustable wing nut C. The quick adjustment is provided in order that the rider may alter the star spring pressure, while riding, to suit the varying road conditions encountered.

Grease Gun Lubrication. A grease-gun is supplied with the kit. To charge this, unscrew the nozzle and press the gun into position in a Tecalemit " EASY FILLING TIN " if available. Now replace the nozzle. To lubricate, place the nozzle of the gun on to the nipple, and by pushing the body of the gun down several times, grease will be forced into the working parts at high pressure. The gun can also be filled by pushing the cork piston to the far end of the gun and inserting grease into the body.

CHAPTER VI

OVERHAULING

Testing and Adjusting Tappet Clearance (S.V. Models). The clearance between the tappets and the valve stems should be checked every 500 miles, though it is unlikely that adjustment will be required unless the valves have been ground-in or a new valve fitted. Always test the clearance with the engine warm, and proceed as follows.

First of all make certain that there is clearance between the bottom exhaust tappet nut and the lifting lever. This indicates that the tappet is in proper contact with the cam. It will be obvious that should the flange on the bottom tappet be resting on the lifter lever, it will prevent the tappet from forming proper contact with the cam inside the timing gear, and only partial valve lift will take place, resulting in loss of power, also speed. Turn the engine round by means of the kick-starter, with the decompressor lever down until compression is felt. Then raise the exhaust lifter and push the kick-starter down another couple of inches, so that the piston is at the top of the compression stroke or thereabouts. Now see if there is any clearance between the valve tappets and valve stems. If the clearance is correct, it should be just possible to feel a little motion when the tappet is lifted up and down with the fingers, and it should be possible to pass a piece of the paper on which this book is printed between the head of the tappet and the valve stem, but a stout visiting card should not go through. If the clearance on either valve is not correct, the tappet must be adjusted. To do this, hold the head A (Fig. 81) by means of the large end of the B.S.A. spanner, and loosen the locking sleeve or nut B with the special tappet spanner provided (turning the handle of the spanner to the left). Then screw the head up or down to the required position, meanwhile holding the stem of the tappet by means of a spanner on the flats C. Then tighten up the locking nut or sleeve B against the tappet nut A. After tightening up, test the clearance again to make sure that it has not been altered inadvertently while tightening up. It is well worth while taking a little trouble over this tappet adjustment, as on its accuracy depends the silence of the valve gear, as well as the power obtained from the engine. On the 9·86 models there is no need to apply a spanner at C, but do not overstrain the locking fillets by which the tappet is prevented from rotating.

OVERHAULING

TAPPET CLEARANCES

Model	Inlet	Exhaust
1·49 h.p. O.H.V.	·004 in.	·006 in.
2·49 h.p. S.V.	·003 in.	·003 in.
2·49 h.p. O.H.V. de Luxe	·003 in.	·003 in.
3·48 h.p. O.H.V. de Luxe	·003 in.	·003 in.
3·48 h.p. O.H.V. Blue Star	·003 in.	·003 in.
4·98 O.H.V. Twin	·002 in.	·008 in.
4·99 h.p. S.V.	·004 in.	·008 in.
4·99 h.p. O.H.V.	·003 in.	·003 in.
4·99 h.p. O.H.V. Blue Star	·003 in.	·003 in.
4·99 h.p. O.H.V. Special	Nil	Nil
5·95 h.p. S.V.	·004 in.	·008 in.
5·95 h.p. O.H.V.	·003 in.	·003 in.
9·86 h.p. S.V.	·004 in.	·008 in.

Valve Clearances on O.H.V. Machines. To ensure quiet valve-gear operation particular attention should always be paid to the clearance between valve and rocker, especially during the first 500 miles (while the working surfaces are bedding down). This should be tested when the engine is cold and with the piston at about top dead-centre at the end of the compression stroke. Test the valve clearance every 500 miles.

To check the valve clearance proceed as follows: Turn the engine round by the kick-starter until compression is felt. Then raise the exhaust lifter and push the kick-starter down another couple of inches so that the piston is at the top of the compression stroke.

There should now be clearance between the rocker and the valve stem. Owing to the pull of the rocker return springs the rocker end should be clear of the valve stem, and if pressure is exerted on the end of the rocker movement should be felt. The clearance should be accurately checked by a set of feeler gauges.

If there is no clearance the valve will never close properly. Starting will be difficult and the face of the valve will become burnt and pitted due to leakage of hot gas at the moment of explosion. If the clearance is excessive the valve gear will be noisy in operation, and loss of power and increased wear will result.

In the case of the exhaust valve first make sure that the valve lifter cam inside the rocker-box is clear of the push-rod flange. It should be possible to operate the exhaust lifter lever through a small angle before moving the rocker, thus showing that the correct clearance exists. If not, the control wire should be adjusted until clearance is obtained.

To Set the Valve Clearance. Remove the rocker-box cover by releasing the spring clip. Undo the locking-nut *A* (Fig. 75) by means of the tappet spanner, and using the small end of the B.S.A. spanner turn the adjusting screw *B* until the correct

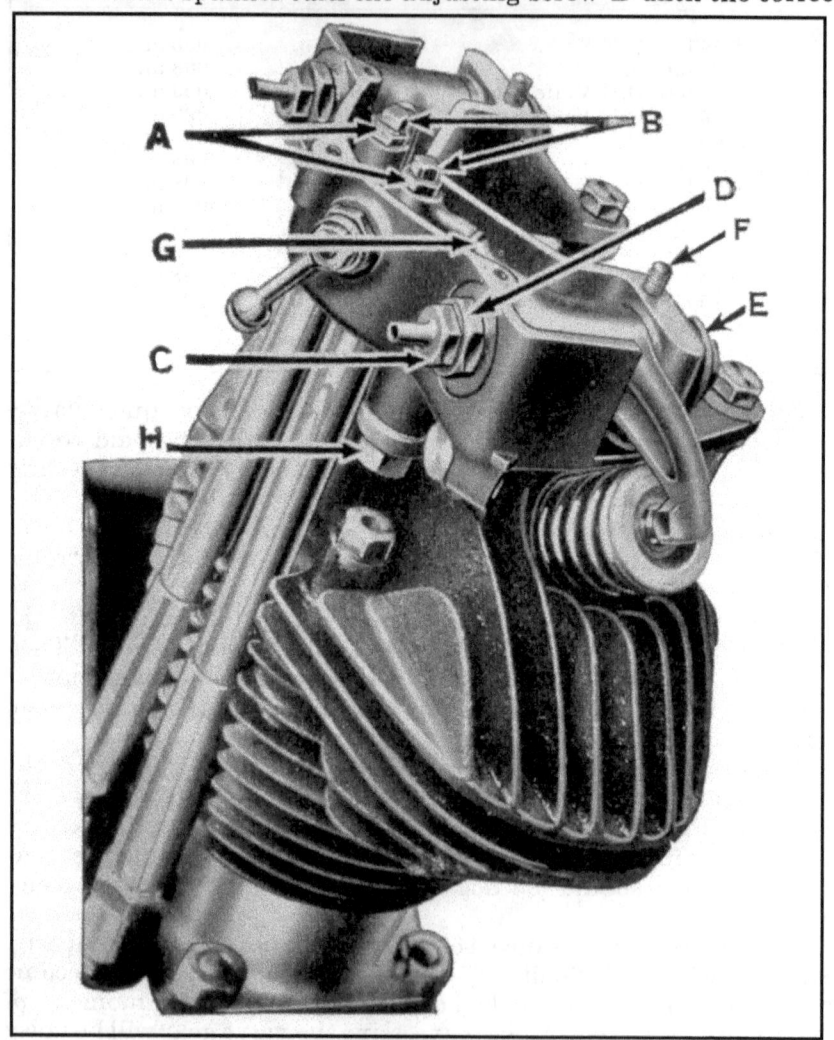

Fig. 75. Valve and Rocker Adjustments

clearance is obtained. Still holding screw *B* tighten the locknut *A*. Check the clearance after tightening the locknut to make certain that this has been done correctly. (See also Fig. 77.)

Adjustment of Rockers. To adjust the overhead rockers for end-play, release locknut *C* (Fig. 75) and turn the adjusting nut *D* to the right until it just becomes tight. Then slacken it back a quarter to one-third of a turn, when play should just be felt when the rocker is shaken end-ways. Then tighten the locknut.

This will be found to be the most accurate way of adjusting the rockers, since the tightening of the locknut takes up the clearance between the threads on the adjusting nut and rocker spindle.

The hexagon E should not be touched during the adjusting process. This must always be screwed up tight, and should only be unscrewed when it is desired to remove the rocker spindle. Before it can be unscrewed the locking stud F should be released by undoing the nut which is screwed on to it.

Lubrication of Rockers. Grease-gun nipples are fitted to the ends of overhead rocker spindles, and lubrication of these points should be carried out every 250 miles or weekly.

Force the grease into the bearing by means of the grease-gun until a large amount oozes out at the ends of the rocker bearing. In this way adequate lubrication for this highly important bearing will be ensured.

Push-rod Ends. The upper push-rod ends should be lubricated once a week. To do this remove the rocker box cover and turn the engine until one of the valves is open. It will then be possible to apply oil to the push-rod end with an oil-can. This should be done for each of the push-rods in turn. Neglect to lubricate these is liable to cause wear and noise.

Oil Mist Lubrication. In addition to the system just described the valve gear is lubricated by oil mist from the engine. Oil mist formed by the splashing action of the flywheels is driven by the descending piston through holes into the timing-case, thence through grooves in the tappet guides, and up the push-rod tubes into the rocker-box. The rockers are fitted with felt rings which accumulate the oil and thus provide additional lubrication for the rocker bearings.

An important advantage of this system is that the valve and rocker gear, being enclosed, are protected from the abrasive action of dust and road grit.

The enclosing of the overhead valve gear, coupled with the efficient lubrication provided, also makes for silent operation.

Return Springs. Return springs are fitted to the push-rods (5·95 h.p. O.H.V. de luxe, 4·99 h.p. O.H.V., 3·49 h.p. O.H.V., and 2·49 h.p. Blue Star Junior).

The push-rod return springs are held between the flange at the bottom of the push-rod and a collar at the top of the lower half of the push-rod tube (see Fig. 80). The latter on the 5·95 h.p.

OVERHAULING

position. These should be removed with a screwdriver. The gauze filter will then come away and the pump can be withdrawn.

To dismantle the pump it is only necessary to remove the four screws in the cover.

On the 2·49 h.p. Blue Star Junior, 3·48 h.p. and 4·99 h.p. models the pump can be removed by unscrewing the four nuts under pump and removing it complete. To dismantle the pump it is only necessary to remove the four screws in the cover. When replacing the 5·95 h.p. pump, make certain that the driving dog on the end of the spindle engages correctly with the slot in the driving spindle.

Decarbonizing the Engine. After 1,500 miles or so have been covered, it may be necessary to decarbonize the engine. The necessity for this will be indicated by the engine becoming very liable to " pink " or knock, particularly when it is hot. To decarbonize the side-valve single-cylinder models it is first necessary to remove the cylinder. Proceed as follows: Unscrew the petrol pipe at the tank end and remove carburettor by undoing the two nuts on the flange and tie this up on the machine out of the way. Detach high-tension lead from sparking plug and remove the latter. Now remove the four nuts which hold the cylinder to the crankcase. Lift the cylinder up and forwards into the front angle of the frame and then turn the engine forwards until the piston comes out of the bottom of the cylinder, steadying the piston as it emerges so that it does not fall over and get damaged when it comes clear of the cylinder.

When removing the cylinder on the twin-cylinder models the procedure is as follows.

Detach the petrol pipe, carburettor, gear control rod, induction pipe union nuts, exhaust pipe union nuts, valve caps, compression taps, and, lastly, the four nuts at the base of each cylinder. Lift cylinder upwards and turn engine until piston is at bottom of stroke, when the cylinder can be entirely removed. The front cylinder can be entirely removed in a similar manner.

On the overhead valve models the cylinder head and barrel are removed as follows.

Unscrew the petrol pipe at the tank end, and remove carburettor by undoing the two nuts on the flange and tie this up on the machine out of the way. Detach high-tension lead from sparking plug and remove the latter. Set the exhaust valve open and disconnect the ball at the end of the Bowden wire from the lifter lever on the rocker-box. Screw out the Bowden wire adjuster to remove it from the rocker-box.

Remove the rocker-box cover and then the rocker-box. The four nuts holding the cylinder head can then be undone. Tap the head lightly and draw it off the studs, removing it from the left-hand side of the machine.

By undoing the four holding-down nuts the cylinder may then be detached. Cover the top of the crankcase with a rag to prevent grit and dust falling in.

Before removing the rocker-box on the 5·95 h.p. O.H.V., it is necessary first to undo the lower push-rod tubes, and lift the push-rod off the tappets with a screwdriver. The push-rods and tubes can then be removed complete. The head is held by five bolts threaded up through the cylinder barrel, and a special

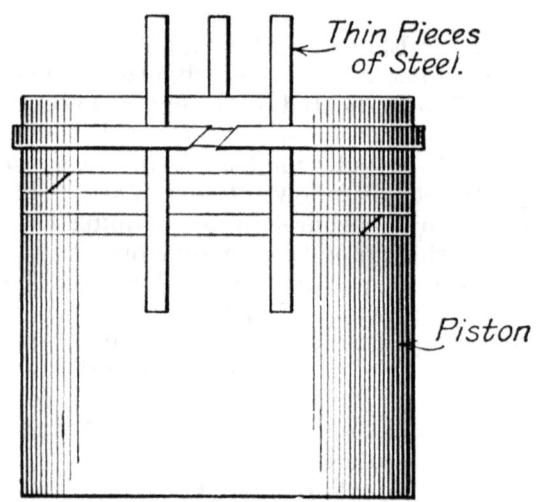

FIG. 82. HOW TO REMOVE PISTON RINGS

spanner is provided to undo these. By undoing the four holding-down nuts the cylinder may then be detached.

Removing the Carbon. Remove the valves from the cylinder and carefully chip out all carbon from the top of the cylinder and the valve pocket and passages with a long-handled screwdriver. After all the carbon has been removed, swill out with paraffin and then wipe the cylinder thoroughly with a clean but oily rag. After scraping carbon off the piston, finish by polishing the top of the piston lightly with fine emery paper or metal polish, taking care not to scratch the side of the cylinder

Examining and Removing Piston Rings. Now examine the piston rings. If they are bright and quite free in their grooves, it is better to leave them alone, as they are very brittle, and there is a considerable risk of breaking them during removal. If there

OVERHAULING

are any brown patches on the rings remove them in the manner shown by Fig. 82, and fit new ones. If the rings are stuck in their grooves, prise them out very carefully and clean them, after soaking in paraffin to soften the carbon. Scrape any carbon from the grooves and from the inside and edges of the rings, and then replace, providing they are otherwise in order. If, however, the machine is used for speed work, the lower piston ring may be discarded with advantage.

Position of Piston Ring Gaps. After cleaning the piston, make sure that the slots in the piston rings are on the opposite sides of the piston to one another, and then smear the sides of the piston generously with engine oil, to obviate any risk of damage when first running after assembly.

PISTON RING GAPS

Model	Gap	
	Minimum	Maximum
2·49 h.p.	·007 in.	·011 in.
3·48 h.p.	·008 in.	·012 in.
4·99 h.p.	·010 in.	·014 in.
5·95 h.p.	·010 in.	·014 in.
9·86 h.p.	·010 in.	·014 in.

Cleaning Out the Crankcase. While the cylinder is off, it is advisable to clean out the crankcase. This is done by unscrewing the drain plug on the bottom right-hand side of the crankcase and allowing the oil to drain out. The crankcase should then be swilled out with paraffin and the plug replaced. Make sure that the latter is screwed up tight.

Reassembling the Engine. After this has been done, the engine may be reassembled. Hold the cylinder in the rear angle of the frame and place the piston a little before bottom dead centre on the downward stroke. The cylinder should then slide home quite easily. Replace the cylinder nuts, making sure they are tight, and then fit the valve caps and compression tap. The carburettor petrol pipe, high tension wire, and exhaust pipe may then be replaced.

Running the Engine after Assembly. Before starting up the engine open the valve fully on the oil sight drip feed fitted to most pre-1933 models, and give at least three complete charges of lubricating oil to the engine. This is very important and must be kept spring plunger can be felt engaging when the lever A is opposite the respective position on the quadrant. The clutch can be adjusted by means of either screw F or G, the lock-nuts having first been released. The screws should then be adjusted until a slight clearance is perceptible between screw F and rod H.

Adjusting the Rear Chain. To adjust the rear chain, loosen the nut on the hub spindle on the left side of the machine; then the nut on the right side. Apply an adjustable spanner (handle upwards) to the square end of the hub spindle, then turn towards the front of the machine until the chain is tight. Slightly turn the reverse way to slacken the chain sufficiently to ensure free running. Hold the spanner firmly in this position, keeping the cams and blocks in close contact, then with the other spanner tighten the left-hand nut, remove the adjustable spanner and tighten up the right-hand spindle nut. This chain should have a sag of about $\frac{1}{2}$ in. when properly adjusted. It may be found necessary to adjust the rear brake after adjusting the rear chain. The models with interchangeable wheels are provided with the usual type of screw chain adjusters.

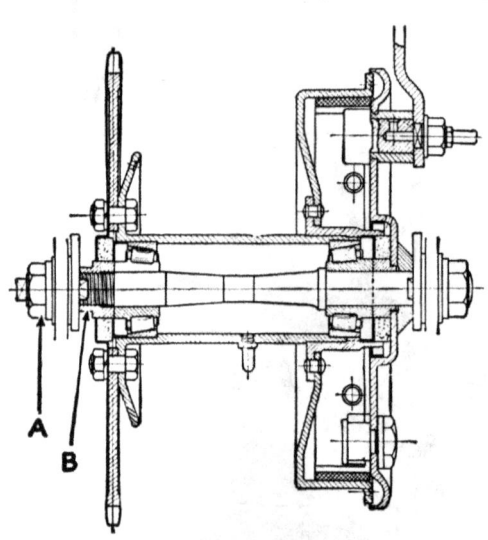

FIG. 87. THE REAR HUB

Hub Adjustment. Both rear and front hubs (shown in section in Figs. 87 and 88 respectively) are of the taper roller bearing type. They should be tested frequently for side-play and adjusted if necessary. To adjust for side-play slacken off the left-hand spindle nut A and turn the bearing nut B gradually, at the same time rotating the wheel slowly and testing for side-play. When the play is all taken up unscrew the nut B about one-third of a turn or until play can just be felt when the wheel is rocked sideways. Upon tightening up the spindle nut A this play will be taken up, and the adjustment will be correct if there is the *barest perceptible shake in the bearing as measured at the wheel rim. Do not srcew the bearing nut B up too tight when making the*

OVERHAULING

preliminary adjustment or the rollers and races may be damaged. On certain 1931 models a lock-nut is fitted adjacent to bearing nut *B* with the object of providing an additional safeguard to the hub adjustment. In the case of machines thus equipped it is necessary to remove the wheels before adjusting the hub bearing.

It is essential that the wheel bearings should be free but without excessive play, and this adjustment should be very carefully made and checked.

On the 1·74 h.p. model (now discontinued) slacken off the nut *A* and turn the left-hand cone *B* (Fig. 88) with the flat cone spanner supplied in the tool kit until the cone becomes tight. Then unscrew the cone about one-third of a turn or until play in the bearing can just be felt when the wheel is rocked sideways. Upon tightening up the spindle nut *A* this play will be taken up, and the adjustment will be correct if there is the barest susceptible shake in the bearing as measured at the wheel rim.

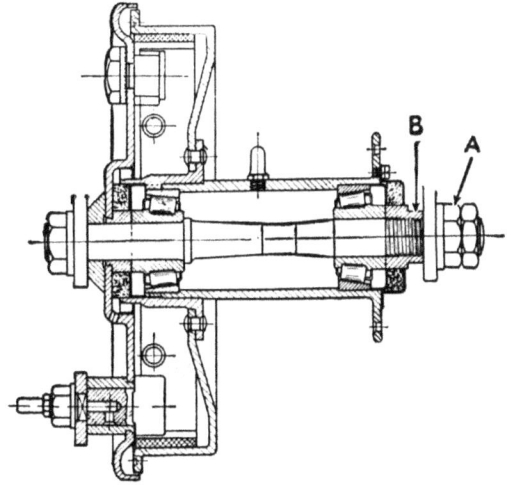

FIG. 88. THE FRONT HUB

It is essential that the bearing should be free, but without excessive play, and this adjustment should, as already stated, be very carefully made and checked.

Brake Adjustment. Quick adjustment is provided for the brakes. To adjust the rear brake it is only necessary to screw the wing-nut fixed to the end of the brake rod backwards or forwards, as the case may be, until the correct setting is obtained.

To adjust the front brake the sleeve mounted on the front fork yoke lug should be screwed in or out. The end of the Bowden cable outer casing fits into this sleeve. The sleeve lock-nut should be released before adjustment and tightened afterwards.

Hub and Brake Lubrication. It is of the utmost importance that the hubs should be greased every 250 miles, or weekly. If this is not done they are liable to overheat and wear. Care should be taken, however, to avoid over-lubricating the hubs, since any excess of grease may reach the brake linings and impair the efficiency of the brakes. When the machines are sent out the hubs are packed with grease, and the regular weekly application of a small quantity will maintain this amount.

The brake cams should be greased every 1,000 miles, or monthly. Only a small quantity of grease should be applied, otherwise the linings may be affected.

Dismantling the Clutch. To dismantle the clutch the nut Y (Fig. 58) must be removed. The end-plate R and spring X will now slide off, leaving the plates accessible. Note the order in which the plates U, V, and W are arranged, so that they can be assembled in the same order (see Figs. 90 and 91). Thoroughly cleanse by

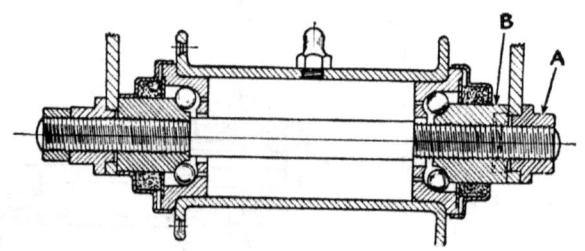

Fig. 89. Diagram Showing how to Adjust the Hub Bearings on the 1·74 h.p. Two-stroke Model (now discontinued)

means of a stiff brush and petrol, removing all trace of oil or grease, and when dry reassemble.

In assembling the clutch the pressure of the spring A (Fig. 90) has to be overcome before the nut B can be engaged on its thread. To enable this to be done a thread has been formed in the nut C, into which the set-screw supplied in the kit may be engaged when the clutch-operating rod has been removed.

It will be seen that by means of the nut D and washer E the nut B may be forced up to the threaded portion F against the pressure of the spring A. When in this position, if the nuts B and D are turned together the former nut will engage on its thread.

Refit cap and make sure that the nuts Z are tight. Instructions for adjusting clutch, control, etc., will be found on the countershaft three-speed and free-engine gear control.

The clutch cable should be greased periodically. This calls for its withdrawal from the outer casing, and the cable should be examined at the ends. If any of the wires are frayed, difficulty will be experienced in re-inserting the cable, and a new one should be fitted. On certain models a somewhat different clutch is fitted, having six springs, but the general instruction is otherwise similar.

OVERHAULING

Cleaning the Machine. The life of the machine is increased and its appearance and value greatly improved by regular and careful attention to cleaning. Especial care should be taken near all moving parts, so as to prevent grit working in and causing undue wear and other troubles. Particularly is this the case

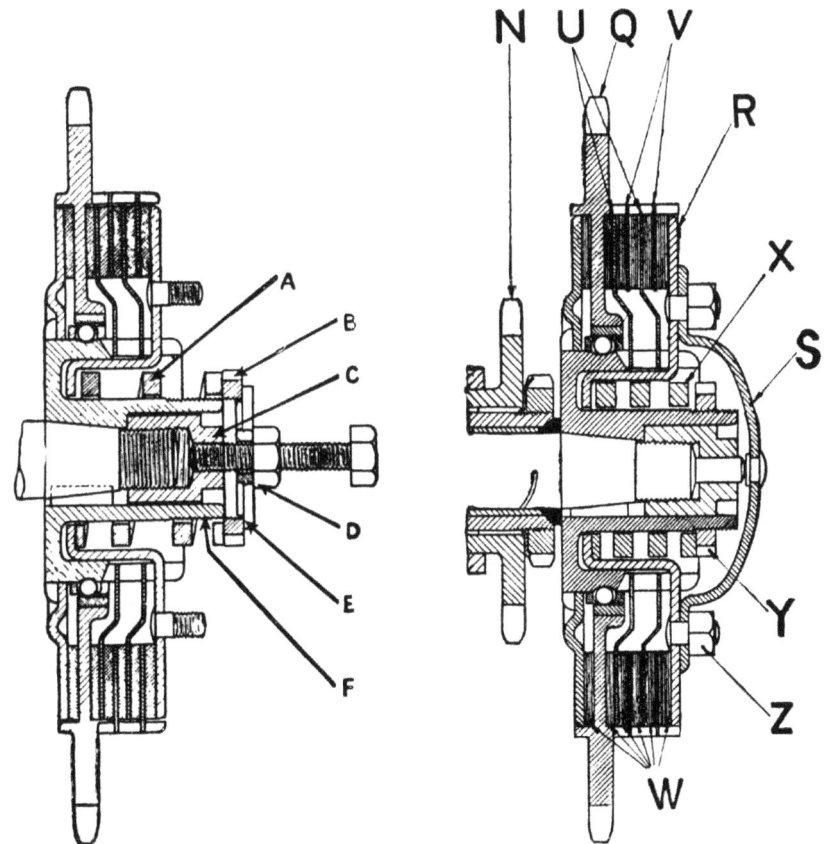

FIGS. 90 AND 91. CROSS-SECTION OF THE
B.S.A. CLUTCH
Showing bolt, nut, and large washer used for
dismantling and assembling the clutch

round the front, rear, and sidecar hubs, carburettor, magneto, valve stems, tappets, front brake and gearbox. Never remove dry and caked mud from the frame, mudguards, etc. To do so means that the enamel will be subjected to the abrasive action of the grit, and the polish will soon be destroyed. Thoroughly soak the dirt first, then wash it off and wipe the parts dry. If a hosepipe is available, this will be found the most satisfactory way of removing dirt. Direct the stream of water on the portion being cleaned, taking care to avoid playing direct on to the hub bearings, etc. Afterwards brush lightly with a soft brush, finally drying and polishing with chamois leather. To remove dirt from the engine, soak it well with paraffin and cleanse with a fresh supply, then wipe dry. To remove oil stains from the crankcase use caustic soda solution. An occasional coating of a cylinder paint should be given to prevent rusting of the cylinder, or a solution of lamp black in paraffin to which a small quantity of gold size has been added may be used. This will also be found to assist the radiation of heat.

The Front Forks. Lubricate the front fork link bearings frequently.

Keep the link bolts tight enough to eliminate side-play, which generally causes a mechanical click. To adjust, unscrew the nuts on the left-hand side and screw up the bolts from the right-hand side just sufficiently tight to eliminate all side play, then lock in position with the nuts, doing one bolt at a time. If too tight, the flexibility of the fork will be reduced.

To Remove the Front Fork Spring. Support the crankcase on a box, so that the front wheel stands clear of the ground. Remove the nut from top spring retaining bolt, and depress same until it can be removed from anchorage lug, afterwards " unwinding " spring from bottom retaining scroll. Then remove the four bolts from the forks by unscrewing the nuts on the left-hand side and withdrawing from the right. Slide out the four links sideways and the forks will fall clear of the machine, and the spring may be lifted off.

The Steering Head. Frequent attention should also be paid to the steering head. A lubricator is fitted on the right-hand side at the bottom of ball head, and thin oil should preferably be used. If this point is not oiled regularly the head will become stiff and the steering will feel unsteady. Therefore oil regularly. To adjust head, unscrew the clip nut, screw down the adjusting nut by means of a special spanner supplied with tool kit until there is no perceptible shake in head, slack back about a twelfth of a turn, and then screw up clip nut again tightly.

Lubricating the Gears. The efficiency and life of the gears will be greatly increased if the following instructions are carefully adhered to. Remove the oil plugs, already referred to, on end plate of gearbox to drain the old oil out, and inject the proper grade of cylinder or gearbox oil until the oil level rises to the top of filler hole when machine is in upright position. This level should be maintained by frequent injections. After every 1,500 miles running, thoroughly flush with paraffin. To do this the machine should be started on the stand, top gear afterwards being engaged with clutch in. Remove the gearbox cover and pour in clean paraffin. With the engine running the gears will be swilled clean, and the paraffin should be drained out by means of the drain plug. Carefully drain by means of the plug provided, afterwards refilling with oil to the correct level. Care should be taken that the clearance between screw *F* and rod *H* (Figs. 57 and 58) is maintained (see instructions for adjusting), otherwise the

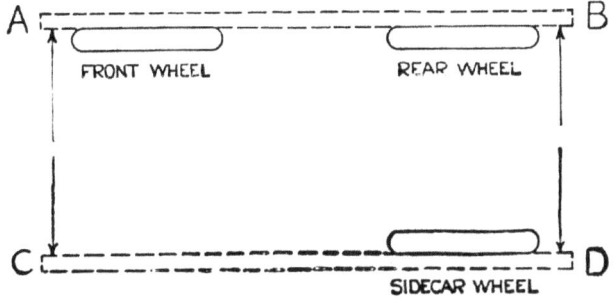

FIG. 91A. HOW TO ALIGN THE SIDECAR

full spring pressure will not be operating on the plates, and clutch will be continually slipping.

Pipe Joints. It is essential that the whole of the joints of the pipes, etc., made between the tank, sight feed, and engine, should be quite airtight, and in the event of a collection of oil in the sight feed which fails to clear itself, the non-return washer, situated under the sight feed, should be inspected. This non-return washer consists of a small pen-steel disc working in a brass socket and prevents blow back from the engine. It will be necessary in this case to ascertain that this has not become displaced, or has been prevented from properly seating itself through dirty or congealed oil. The parts in question should be cleaned and the final delivery pipe should also be inspected for a partial stoppage when this trouble will, without doubt, be overcome.

Alignment of the B.S.A. Sidecar. The 3·48 h.p. and higher powered models only are designed for a sidecar, connections being formed integral with the frame.

It is essential for the life of the machine that the sidecar is correctly aligned, and Fig. 91A shows how this should be carried out. Lay a long wooden straight edge (*A–B*) along both wheels of the motor-bicycle, and a similar straight edge (*C–D*) along the sidecar wheel. Make certain that the machine is perfectly upright; then adjust the sidecar until the points A and C are ½ in. closer together than the points B and D.

For the purpose of alignment, the main sidecar connection is provided with adjusting washers, two of which are at the chassis end of the main front arm and four on the footboard connection. These are supplied loose and are to be used in lining up the machine, if necessary, to obtain the correct alignment as in the diagram.

The rear connection is fitted with spherical washer and spring

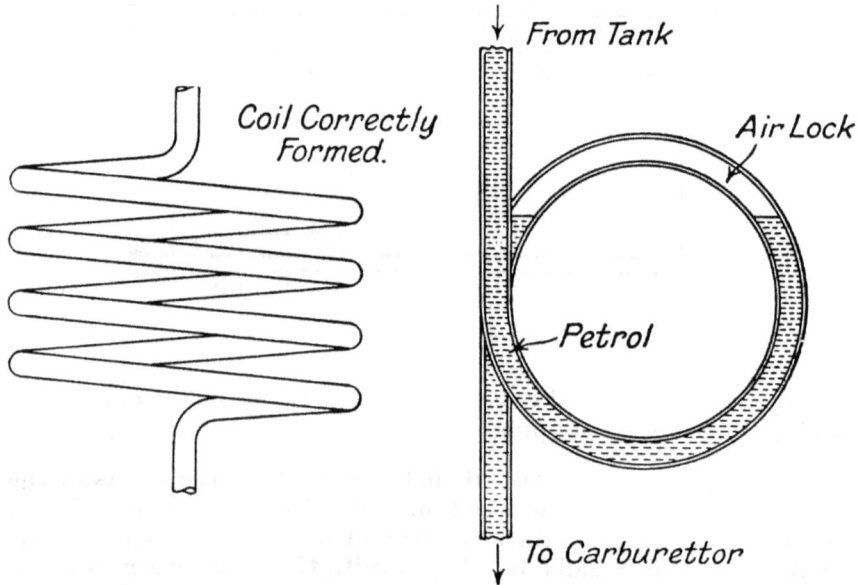

FIGS. 92 AND 93. THE CORRECT AND INCORRECT METHODS OF COILING PETROL PIPES

washer to facilitate the vertical alignment of the machine. Lock up tightly after the correct alignment has been obtained. It is important that any vertical alignment should be released at the bolts on the twin tubes of the chassis.

Care should be taken to refit all castellated nuts with split cotter pins.

Coiling Petrol Pipes. Figs. 92 and 93 show the correct and incorrect methods of forming the coils in petrol pipes. It will be noticed that an air lock (a common trouble) is caused when the coils are formed with a horizontal axis. They should, of course, have a vertical axis.

OVERHAULING

Removing Tight Studs. Fig. 94 shows the method of removing studs for purposes of replacement. Two nuts are locked together, and a spanner used on the *bottom* one to unscrew the stud.

Paper Washers. These are useful in preventing leakage, and may be made by placing a sheet of paper over the part for which the washer is intended and rubbing round the edge. A clear impression is thus made on the paper.

Truing Wheels. The preliminary operation is first to ascertain the extent of warp or deviation from the circular, and this is

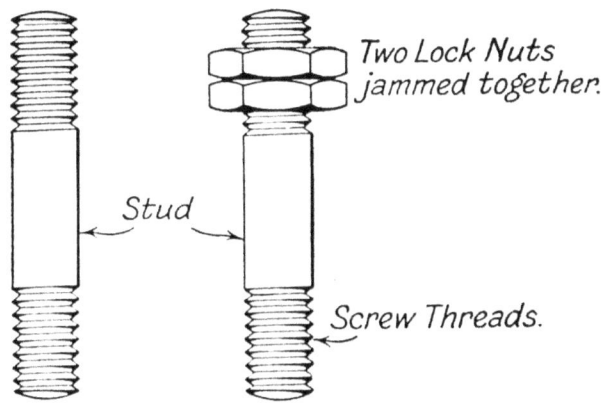

FIG. 94. HOW TO REMOVE STUDS

done by spinning the rim between the forks, holding a piece of chalk to the rim, so that the hit-and-miss places are clearly marked. Where the rim rises and falls, the spokes at those parts must be respectively tightened or slackened. If the wheel is " out of flat " (lack of truth sideways) the spokes must be tightened on one side and loosened on the other. It is a fiddling operation requiring great care. A nipple key should be used for turning the nipples.

Having trued the wheels sideways and circumferentially, pass a cord through the spokes and stretch it taut so that it lies diagonally across the oil-hole of the hub, and also touches the rim on opposing sides. Next reverse the position of the diagonal, so that it touches the other two opposing sides. If the wheel is not pulled over on the hub, the string should pass over the centre of the oil-hole in both instances.

The spokes when plucked with the fingers should all yield the same note. If at any time it is necessary to remove the rim from the spokes, perhaps to change rims or remove a dent, and the rider is uncertain about wheel building, before removing the nipples obtain some fine copper wire and tie the spokes together at the point where they intercept one another. Then remove the nipples and carefully spring the spokes out of place, which will leave them in their proper position on the hub.

Re-enamelling. With so many excellent enamels on the market, the amateur can obtain excellent results if at the time of overhauling he considers the frame needs enamelling. If time and expense warrant it, he is, however, advised to have it stoved, a special process of *baking* the enamel on, which cannot be done at home without special plant. The frame should be stripped of fittings and scraped down to the bare metal with an old knife, or the edge of a piece of glass, and then polished absolutely bright and smooth with emery cloth. This is important, for any imperfections in the surface, such as roughness or rust, will affect the finished surface. The modern cellulose finishes are also recommended.

Then give a coat of enamel of the desired colour. When this is thoroughly dry, dull its surface with very fine glasspaper, and apply a second coat. Repeat this process until four or five coats have been applied, when a coat of varnish should be evenly brushed on and left to get thoroughly hard.

The work should be carried out in a warm room or shed, and when applying the varnish, the floor should be sprinkled with water to lay the dust.

The varnish should be left to dry, keeping doors and windows shut to exclude all dust, which, if allowed to enter, will settle on the varnish, causing the latter to dry with a gritty surface.

Lining transfers are on the market, and if used should be applied before the coat of varnish.

Front Fork. Keep the top link bolts just tight enough to eliminate side-play, which generally causes a mechanical click when the machine is rocked sideways. To adjust, unscrew the nuts on the left-hand side and screw up the bolts from the right-hand side just sufficiently tight to eliminate all side-play, then lock in position with the nuts, doing one bolt at a time. If too tight the flexibility of the fork will be reduced. It should be noted that the links on the right-hand side have plain holes and those on the left have threaded holes.

Shock Absorber. This device is incorporated with the bottom fork link to enable the deflection and rebound of the fork on rough roads to be controlled. The amount of damping is adjusted by the wing-nut on the right-hand lower front fork bolt. On certain of the 1935 models, to adjust the amount of friction, first slack off the rear nut on left side or fork. Then screw up or unscrew the bolt to give more or less friction as required, finally locking up the left-hand nut again. The bottom fork link bolt should be adjusted similarly to the top link bolts.

To Remove Front Fork Spring and Forks. Support the crankcase on a box so that the front wheel hangs clear of the ground. Remove the nut from top spring retaining bolt and depress same until it can be removed from anchorage lug, afterwards "unwinding" spring from bottom retaining scroll. Then remove the four bolts from the forks by unscrewing the nuts on the left-hand side and withdrawing from the right. Slide out the four links sideways and the forks will fall clear of the machine. To adjust the head it is first of all necessary to slacken the steering damper right back. Then unscrew the clip-nut, screw down the adjusting nut by means of a special spanner supplied with tool kit until there is no perceptible shake in head, slack down about a twelfth of a turn, and then screw up clip-nut again tightly.

Steering Damper. A B.S.A. steering damper is fitted on models other than B331 and B332 (1934) to the lower end of the steering stem yoke, and the pressure is adjustable by means of a knob mounted on the top of the steering head. The function of a steering damper is two fold. In the case of solo machines it ensures stability at high speeds on rough roads and prevents "speed wobble." When fitted to a sidecar combination a steering damper eliminates the tendency to "handlebar wobble" and reduces steering drag. The steering damper should be adjusted to suit individual requirements. Beyond occasional cleaning of the friction discs the B.S.A. damper requires no attention.

Hub Adjustment. The hubs on the 2·49 h.p. S.V. and 2·49 h.p. O.H.V. (1934) are of the ball-bearing cup-and-cone type, but adjustment is made in the same way as with the taper-roller bearing hubs following. Both front and rear hubs on the 2·49 h.p. O.H.V. Blue Star and larger models are of the taper roller bearing type. They should be tested frequently for side-play and adjusted if necessary. To adjust for side-play remove the wheel and then slacken off the locknut A (Fig. 88) and turn the bearing nut B gently. When the play is all taken up, unscrew the nut B about one-third of a turn or until play can just be felt when the spindle is rocked sideways. Upon tightening the locknut A, see that this play is not all taken up. The adjustment will be correct if there is the barest perceptible shake in the bearing as measured at the wheel rim. When the wheel is replaced do not screw the bearing nut B up too tight when making the preliminary adjustment or the roller and races may be damaged. It is essential that the wheel bearings should be free but without excessive play, and this adjustment should be very carefully made and checked.

Detachable Rear Wheel—1935 Models. Many 1935 models are fitted with a quickly detachable rear wheel. To remove the wheel it is only necessary to unscrew the wheel bolt *C* on the right-hand

FIG. 95. DETACHING THE FRONT WHEEL

side of the hub and draw this nearly out. Then, using the projecting bolt as a handle, slide it to the rear carrying with it the distance piece *D*. When this is drawn clear, the wheel should be moved bodily to the right until it clears the driving dogs. It can be withdrawn to the rear. Adjustment of the wheel bearing is carried out in a manner similar to that just described in the hub adjustment, except that while the adjustment is being made the hollow spindle must be held by a spanner on the flats *E* (Fig. 95).

Detachable Wheels—9·86 h.p. Models. To detach the rear wheel (Fig. 96) place the machine on the stand, withdraw bolt *A* and remove distance-piece *B*. Pull the wheel gently towards the right hand side of the machine, when it will drop out of engagement with the serrated chain wheel. In replacing the wheel thoroughly clean the serrations on both hub shell and chain wheel and well coat both with vaseline or thick grease. To detach the front wheel, slacken off the nuts (Fig. 95) sufficiently far to allow the stand to be knocked down. Then raise the machine on the stand. Release the locknut B, and unscrew the toggle-pin C. Now unscrew the nut D, preventing the bolt E from turning by means of the adjustable spanner. Pull out the bolt and the wheel will

FIG. 96. DETACHING THE REAR WHEEL

be free to drop out. Be careful not to lose the distance-piece which goes between the hub and the wheel bracket on the left-hand side of the machine. The brake cover-plate and drum should be removed and attached to the new wheel when changing wheels. To replace the front wheel, first see that the brake is pushed home on the splines and then lift it into position. Hold the wheel so that the brake cover-plate stud is engaged in the slot on the inner side of the wheel bracket at F, and push the bolt E partly through the hub. Before pushing the bolt right through, place the distance-piece mentioned above in position. Then push the bolt right through and screw up the nut D. Replace the toggle-pin C and locknut B. Finally push the machine off the stand and refix the latter in position.

Lubrication of Rear Hub Chainwheel Bearing. After detaching the rear wheel as previously described, the hole E should be filled with thick grease, then when reassembling wheel in position, on screwing up the bolt A the grease is forced up the passage F to the ball-races.

Hub Adjustment. Remove the wheel from the machine, and, holding the flats on B with the adjustable spanner supplied in the tool kit, unscrew the locknut A at the other end of the hub (see Figs. 95 and 96). Note that this has a left-hand thread and unscrews to the right. Remove the locking-washer C and screw the nut D (left-hand thread) in or out until the correct adjustment is obtained. This is best done by turning nut D until it is just tight and then unscrewing about a third of a turn. Replace the locking-washer, making sure that the peg in the nut D engages with one of the holes in the washer. If necessary, move the nut a little either way or turn the washer upside down to enable the peg to engage. When this is done replace the locknut A and tighten up.

Brake Adjustment. Quick adjustment is provided for the brakes. To adjust the rear brake it is only necessary to screw the wing-nut fixed to the end of the brake rod backwards or forwards, as the case may be, until the correct setting is obtained. To adjust the front brake the sleeve mounted on the front fork yoke lug should be screwed in or out. The end of the cable outer casing fits this sleeve. The sleeve locknut should be released before adjustment and tightened afterwards.

Coupled Brakes. Directly coupled brakes are fitted on all models except the 2·49 h.p. S.V. and O.H.V. Single Port and 9·86 h.p. twin. Each brake is provided with separate adjustment as described above. There is, however, a further adjustment by means of which the coupling between front and rear can be regulated. This is situated just above the brake pedal. The most satisfactory results will be obtained if the coupling is adjusted with both wheels on their stands. The coupling adjustor should then be screwed up or down until both brakes come into operation simultaneously.

Carburettor Jet Sizes. On the smaller models the fitting of an air cleaner has little or no effect on carburation, and no alteration is therefore made to the jet size. Should it be felt, however, that the mixture is slightly rich when an air cleaner is used a jet one size smaller should be tried. On the 4·99 h.p. and 5·95 h.p. model a jet three sizes smaller is required when an air cleaner is fitted. The jet fitted to the carburettor when the machine is sent out is suitable for normal running. For extra heavy work one size larger may be used, while if extreme economy is necessary a jet one size smaller than that fitted should be employed.

Compression. The engine compression should be tested regularly. This should be such that a definite resistance to movement is encountered when the kick-starter is depressed. If the latter can be pushed down easily without the exhaust lifter being raised it is an indication that the compression is faulty, and the matter should be investigated farther. If the engine compression is faulty this may be due to leakage past the sparking plug washer or past the piston rings and valves. Lack of compression may also be due to a defective cylinder head joint washer. If the sparking plug is loose, smear the washer with oil and tighten. The presence of any defect in the washer itself will then be indicated by bubbles when the kick-starter is depressed. If the washer is faulty fit a new one. The valve clearance should be carefully checked to see that the valves are properly seated. If there is no clearance the valves should be removed for examination, when it may be found that the seatings are pitted or the valves are burned. Badly pitted valves should be reground and valves which are burned should be replaced. It is extremely important that the valve clearances should be correct, since running without clearance always results in serious damage to the valves. The most convenient way to test the cylinder head washer without removing the head is to place the machine on the stand and start up the engine. Hold the back of the hand close to the cylinder in line with the joint. Any "blow" past the washer will be felt by the hand. Test all round the joint in this way. If the washer is still suspected, even although this test fails to reveal any defect, examination of the washer will show definitely whether or not leakage occurs at this joint. The presence of black patches on the washer will indicate that the joint is defective. The cylinder head bolts should be tightened down periodically to prevent leakage developing at the washer. The piston rings should also be examined as described under the heading "Piston and Rings." The width of the gap is important. If this is excessive leakage may occur, and new rings should be fitted. Should leakage still occur even when new rings are fitted, examine the cylinder bore. This may be scored or badly worn, due to under-lubrication. In this case it may be necessary to have the cylinder bore reground and to fit an oversize piston.

To Remove Engine from Frame. In order to do this it is necessary to detach chain-cases and chains on all but models B331 and B332, the clutch complete, the exhaust pipes, the carburettor, exhaust lifter cable, and the rocker-box. Slacken off the bolt connecting the cylinder torque stay, if fitted, to the frame lug, and swing the stay clear. The bolts which hold the crankcase in the frame should then be withdrawn, and the engine can be lifted out from the left side of the machine.

Compression Ratios and Fuels. The compression ratios of the O.H.V. models are tabulated below.

Model	Compression Ratio	
	Standard	With Shim
2·49 h.p. O.H.V. Single Port	6·0	—
2·49 h.p. O.H.V. Blue Star	6·9	6·3
3·48 h.p. O.H.V.	6·4	—
3·48 h.p. Blue Star	6·8	6·4
4·99 h.p. O.H.V.	5·8	5·4
4·99 h.p. O.H.V. Blue Star	6·9	6·4
4·99 h.p. O.H.V. Special	7·5	6·8
5·95 h.p. O.H.V.	5·5	—

The best fuel for use in the "Blue Star" and special models is a mixture of 50 per cent benzol and 50 per cent No. 1 petrol. Aviation spirit may be used in place of the latter for special work. For touring, the benzol mixtures and fuels containing lead compounds which are now available are quite satisfactory. The standard engines, both S.V. and O.H.V., can be run on any "straight" petrol. It is, however, advisable always to use a reputable brand of No. 1 grade in order to obtain maximum results.

CHAPTER VII

TOURING

MOTOR-cycle touring to-day is almost as certain as travelling by railway, and is, if anything, less costly and certainly much healthier. There is the added pleasure of being able to vary one's rate of progress at will—lingering amongst pleasant scenery and hurrying through the drab portions. The important questions are those of dress, luggage, tools, equipment, maps and guides.

DRESS

Personal comfort is of first importance, and all the delights of the weather and the countryside are liable to be lost sight of if it is not attained. It is wise to remember the humour and even contempt with which a certain type of motor-cyclist is regarded. You know the sort—the owner of one of the lightest of lightweights who will dash round the country at the alarming rate of about 12 miles an hour, clad in a heavy leather suit, goggles, heavy crash helmet and Wellingtons. Do not follow his example. Select your dress with due regard to utility, comfort and appearance. There is little need to provide special clothing for pottering. Protection from dust is all that is needed, and a light coat of the dustproof variety fills the bill. Apart from penetrating one's clothing, dust can also produce painful results if a sharp piece gets under the eyelids, and for this reason goggles are an essential part of the equipment. One's ordinary clothes may be used, but there is always the risk of splashing them with oil, or otherwise spoiling them. It is cheaper in the long run, if a great deal of riding is to be done, to have a special dress consisting of riding breeches and leggings or stockings, the dustproof coat (of the sports coat type), and goggles.

Goggles. A word or so here about goggles is advisable. Goggles are obtainable in a variety of forms, from the one-piece celluloid pattern to the spectacle type having two oval lenses, which may be replaced when broken. The former, the writer finds, are extremely comfortable to wear, and as well the field of vision is not so restricted as with the lens type. Goggles with tinted glasses are also available, and in bright sunlight are extremely restful to the eyes. One has only to ride with the sun glaring in one's eyes for any distance to realize what "sun-blindness" is, and the feeling of helplessness which accompanies it.

These coloured glasses (blue and yellow are useful colours) lessen the possibility of this.

Another type of goggles which has the laudable object of saving the eyes of the rider in the event of accident is the Triplex goggles. Each lens of this consists of two layers of glass with a layer of celluloid between, and although in the case of an accident they may crack, they do not actually break.

There is another point connected with goggles which receives all too little attention. It is the *fit* of them. Goggles which do not fit closely to the face will cause colds in the eyes and eye soreness, and even dust may enter the eye. See to it, then, that the goggles fit close to the face.

All Weather Riding. Whilst it cannot be disputed that spring and summer riding is pleasanter, autumn and winter riding, providing the day is not wet, is not without its charm.

Winter clothing is certainly on a more elaborate scale than summer clothing. Underclothing, which in summer is of the light " summer-weight " variety, should be of the heavy woollen winter quality. The commonest type of winter dress, and one which withal is the cheapest, consists of the ordinary buff waterproof coat and leggings, the latter lacing or buttoning up the sides. They may be purchased from most accessory dealers. An objection to them is that they soon show grease marks, and even when fitting nicely lack that smart appearance which the average motor cyclist requires. Another objection is the awkward operation of lacing or buttoning the leggings, especially if the fingers are cold.

A much more satisfactory " all weather " apparel consists of a brown oilskin coat, of such a length that it barely covers the knees. To have it longer is to make kick-starting awkward, and to run the risk of portions getting caught in the transmission or spokes. Two patterns are made—one which buttons together and one which straps together. The writer prefers the latter, as it is possible to pull it more closely to the body, under which condition it is warmer and excludes penetrating draughts.

The apparel for the legs to be worn with the oilskin for winter riding may consist of that already recommended, but undoubtedly the best form of mud and water excluder is a pair of waders, which somewhat resemble fishermen's waders. They may appear ungainly, but they do keep one dry, and enable one to arrive at the destination clean and dry underneath, and there is no risk of the trousers becoming soiled.

Overall suits of light material enable one's ordinary attire to be worn underneath, and upon arriving at the home of, say, one's sweetheart, it is merely necessary to remove the overalls to present a spick and span appearance. If anything, they are more suited to summer riding, but plenty of riders wear them all the year round.

Headwear. The writer considers that, for headwear, a cap is most satisfactory, and it should be of such a fit that it may be worn peak to the front, with little risk of being blown off. Some riders wear caps peak to the back, for one of two reasons. Either the cap is too large and blows off when correctly worn, or they wish in their vanity to be regarded as racing motor cyclists. The peak helps to keep the sun from the eyes, and its only objection is that it is in the way when raising the goggles.

A felt hat of the soft, or trilby, pattern is comfortable if of good fit, and is cooler to wear in summer than a cap.

The helmet undoubtedly is advisable for those who intend to ride long distances in all weathers, for while it must be admitted that some wear them to " look the part," it is entirely wrong to assume that only racing men should wear them. They are preferred because they are extremely comfortable in use, eliminate the whistle of the wind past one's ears when travelling in a wind or at fairly high speed, are quite weatherproof, and do not blow off. Helmets of the crash type are intended for competition work, and for such are advised. Those likely to have much riding to do in wet weather may find the fisherman's " sou'-wester," perhaps, even more serviceable than a helmet.

Several other garments are marketed. Woollen cardigans, having long sleeves, and intended to be worn in conjunction with sleeved leather waistcoats are excellent as aids to warmth. In all cases avoid the loud extreme, if you do not wish to be a standing joke among your friends.

Gloves. The problem of keeping the hands warm and at the same time enabling them to finger the controls sensitively, is a difficult one. Ordinary fleece-lined gloves allow the air to blow up the sleeve. To obviate this, gauntlets may be worn. These have an extension which fits over the coat sleeve. The difficulty with gloves and gauntlets, however, is that the fingers " fumble " the controls, and are not nearly so sensitive.

The writer does not recommend woollen gloves, for they are liable to become caught in the controls and, say, drag the throttle lever open at the very moment when it is desired to be closed.

An attempt to solve the glove difficulty has been made by one or two firms who market a rubber muff, like the extension of the gauntlet glove. This fits over and beyond the grips of the handle-bars, so that the hands are sheltered and the wind deflected.

Leg Shields. The obvious object of these is to keep the clothing clean and dry, and in muddy weather they undoubtedly do keep a considerable amount off, but the very wide and efficient mudguarding of the B.S.A. machine renders their use almost unnecessary. Shields usually screw on to the footboards and clip on to the frame.

Windscreens. Handlebar windscreens have been marketed which attach to the handlebars and prevent the face from getting cold.

LUGGAGE

The question of what luggage to carry on a tour depends to a great extent on the length of the tour and the type of machine. The point of view to adopt is : What can I do without ? Not : What can I do with ?

For a week-end tour one obviously must take night attire, a clean shirt and vest, two clean collars (to provide a margin for accidents with greasy fingers), shaving tackle, tooth brush, brush and comb, soft hat or cap, and socks. With regard to clothing, although space may be found for it, it is well to travel in the suit one desires to wear, and to protect it in the manner already noted under " Dress." It must be remembered that on a solo machine only a small suit case can be accommodated, as only the carrier is available for it, but with a sidecar, even though a passenger be carried, there is the additional space afforded by the locker, and small items can easily be accommodated in with the passenger. All bags should be packed as tightly as possible to avoid damage by road vibration.

If the tour is to last for a week or a fortnight, carry only sufficient clothing for immediate needs, and arrange for underclothing, etc., to be sent on to an appropriate destination, returning the soiled apparel by the same means.

INCIDENTAL MATTERS

Spares. There is little need to carry more than a repair outfit, pump, usual tools, as supplied with the machine, spare plugs, spare tubes, spare chains (and spare chain links) and chain extractor or belt punch, and spare valves and valve springs.

Useful oddments such as cones, bolts, nuts, chain-coupling links, insulating tape, electric bulbs and/or burners can be packed in a small box with pieces of rag stuffed between to prevent rattle and damage

Maps and Guides. These are quite a necessary adjunct to touring, and, indeed, the fascination of planning a tour is part of its pleasure. The route should be traced out in red ink on the map, and the sidecar passenger is then able to direct the driver by following the map in conjunction with the direction taken. A contour road book is useful, in that it enables one to pick the flattest route. Ordnance survey maps are recommended, or Bartholomew's, and a scale of one mile or two miles to the inch is preferred. So complete and comprehensive are these maps that finding one's way is simplicity itself. It should here be mentioned that Messrs. Michelin publish an excellent road guide almost indispensable to the tourist, for in it is a list of the hotels and repairers for every village and town in the United Kingdom. Additionally, the distance from one town to another is given, and street plans of important towns are presented. It is a wonderful compilation, deservedly popular and quite interesting to read. The Dunlop Tyre Company issue a work of equal merit, and either of the volumes can be recommended.

The Tour in Prospect. If the reader is considering a tour and is a member of one of the Associations mentioned in Chapter II, it is well to remember that these offer special touring facilities to their members, and accordingly the secretary should be apprised of the intended route. Especially is this necessary when a continental tour is to be undertaken, for the Society sees to the obtaining of the members' passports, carnets or triptiques, and renders unnecessary the leaving of deposits when going into a foreign land to satisfy legal requirements regarding the law of imports and exports.

Taking the Machine Abroad. The triptique referred to in the last paragraph enables the owner to travel in Finland, Holland, France, Italy, Switzerland, Belgium, Portugal, Spain, Rumania, Russia, Norway and Sweden, or as an alternative he can be equipped with an International Customs Pass, issued by the A.C.U. and A.A. to members and non-members, whereby the highest continental duty payable suffices for all the countries forming part of the Convention.

International Travelling Passes (lasting 12 months) are also issued, enabling the holders to travel in all countries which are parties to the agreement, without obtaining special licences or carrying special numbers in each country as hitherto. The Customs Pass concerns the customs duty payable ; the Travelling Pass is exclusively a licence for the machine and driver abroad.

Up-to-date information about the best means of transit and the best routes is also supplied, and may save a lot of trouble.

It is not nowadays required of the tourist to submit to being examined by a foreign official, to obtain foreign licences,

LIGHTING-UP TIMES—APRIL, 1935, TO MARCH, 1936

Date	ENGLAND AND WALES							SCOTLAND				
	London	Bir-m'gham	Cardiff	Exeter	Leeds	Man-chester	Nor-wich	Edin-burgh	Glas-gow	Inver-ness	Thurso
Apr. 7, 1935	7.15	7.25	7.28	7.28	7.26	7.28	7.12	7.36	7.40	7.43	7.43
" 14, "	8.57	9.07	9.10	9.09	9.09	9.11	8.55	9.20	9.24	9.28	9.29
" 28, "	9.21	9.31	9.34	9.32	9.35	9.37	9.19	9.49	9.52	9.59	10.01
May 12, "	9.44	9.45	9.55	9.53	9.58	10.00	9.42	10.15	10.19	10.28	10.32
" 26, "	10.01	10.14	10.14	10.25	10.19	10.20	10.02	10.39	10.43	10.54	11.00
June 9, "	10.15	10.28	10.28	10.25	10.35	10.36	10.17	10.56	11.00	11.13	11.20
" 23, "	10.21	10.34	10.34	10.31	10.41	10.42	10.23	11.03	11.07	11.21	11.28
July 7, "	10.16	10.29	10.29	10.27	10.35	10.36	10.17	10.56	11.00	11.12	11.19
" 21, "	10.03	10.15	10.16	10.13	10.19	10.21	10.03	10.37	10.41	10.52	10.57
Aug. 4, "	9.41	9.53	9.54	9.53	9.56	9.59	9.40	10.13	10.17	10.24	10.26
" 18, "	9.15	9.25	9.28	9.27	9.27	9.29	9.13	9.40	9.44	9.49	9.50
Sept. 1, "	8.44	8.54	8.57	8.57	8.54	8.56	8.41	9.05	9.09	9.12	9.12
" 15, "	8.12	8.21	8.25	8.26	8.20	8.22	8.08	8.28	8.32	8.33	8.32
" 29, "	7.40	7.48	7.53	7.54	7.45	7.48	7.34	7.51	7.55	7.54	7.50
Oct. 6, "	7.24	7.32	7.37	7.39	7.28	7.31	7.18	7.33	7.37	7.35	7.30
" 20, "	5.24	5.30	5.37	5.40	5.25	5.29	5.17	5.28	5.32	5.28	5.21
Nov. 3, "	4.57	5.03	5.10	5.13	4.56	5.00	4.49	4.55	4.59	4.53	4.45
" 17, "	4.37	4.41	4.50	4.54	4.34	4.38	4.28	4.31	4.35	4.27	4.17
Dec. 1, "	4.24	4.28	4.37	4.42	4.19	4.24	4.14	4.15	4.19	4.08	3.56
" 15, "	4.22	4.25	4.35	4.39	4.15	4.20	4.11	4.09	4.13	4.01	3.49
" 29, "	4.29	4.33	4.42	4.47	4.23	4.28	4.19	4.17	4.21	4.10	3.58
Jan. 11, 1936	4.47	4.50	5.00	5.04	4.42	4.47	4.37	4.38	4.42	4.32	4.21
" 25, "	5.10	5.14	5.23	5.27	5.08	5.11	5.01	5.06	5.09	5.02	4.53
Feb. 8, "	5.35	5.41	5.48	5.51	5.36	5.29	5.27	5.36	5.39	5.34	5.27
" 22, "	6.01	6.07	6.14	6.15	6.04	6.07	5.54	6.06	6.10	6.07	6.01
Mar. 7, "	6.26	6.33	6.39	6.39	6.30	6.33	6.20	6.36	6.40	6.39	6.35
" 21, "	6.38	6.45	6.51	6.51	6.43	6.46	6.32	6.50	6.54	6.54	6.51

Summer Time in 1935 commences at 2 a.m., 14th April; and ends at 2 a.m, 6th October.
In 1936 Summer Time commences at 2 a.m., 19th April; and ends at 2 a.m, 4th October.

temporary foreign numbers, or any other of the onerous formalities. It is only necessary to obtain the International pass, and fix an oval plate to the machine with the letters G.B. painted in white on a black ground. This plate must be illuminated at night.

Continental Rule of the Road, etc. As a general rule *Keep to the Left* and *Pass on the Right* in Austria, Hungary, Portugal and Sweden.

As a general rule *Keep to the Right* and *Pass on the Left* in Belgium, France, Germany, Holland, Italy, Russia, Spain, Switzerland, and also in Carinthia (Austria), Carniola, Dalmatia, Istria, and Tyrol.

The speed limit in Belgium is 40 kilom. an hour in the country, and 15 in town. Special regulations apply to Brussels. Motor-cycles may use the paths made specially for cyclists. The Belgian roads (except in some districts) are exceedingly bad.

Lamps must be lit in France not later than fifteen minutes after sunset. A *green* light, in the case of motor-cars, should be shown in front on the left, and it is compulsory to carry an efficient tail light on the left-hand side to illuminate clearly the back number plates at night time.

Normally the majority of French roads are very good. Cars and motor-cycles entering Paris are stopped, the petrol in the tanks is measured, and *octroi* duty charged.

The roads in Holland are generally good, but narrow and winding. No speed limit is fixed on country roads, but motorists can be charged with driving to the common danger. Some roads are closed to motor traffic.

The general rule of the road in Italy is to keep to the right, but it is frequently reversed in many districts and in many towns.

In Northern Italy and parts of Central Italy, the roads are good and sometimes excellent; in the Southern Provinces the roads are bad.

The speed limit in Spain is 12 kilom. ($7\frac{1}{4}$ miles) per hour.

CHAPTER VIII

FAULTS: THEIR LOCATION AND REMEDY

THE four tables given on succeeding pages afford a convenient method of tracing faults. It requires considerable experience to be able quickly to diagnose the cause of trouble. The beginner must not think from the rather lengthy list that a motor-cycle is always likely to be in trouble. It is only very occasionally that trouble arises.

Some riders have a tendency always to be adjusting and improving the running of the engine. When the engine is running well it is wise to leave it alone.

IGNITION TROUBLES

Testing the Plugs. If it is considered that the engine does not need taking down, yet it is difficult to start, examine the plug, and, holding it by means of the cable (don't hold the plug body with the fingers, for if the plug is defective, a mild but unpleasant shock will speedily make you aware of the fact when the engine is kicked over) so that its metal body touches the cylinder, turn the engine over by means of the kick-starter and note whether the spark is regular and " fat." An intermittent spark, or a regular but weak " pin-point " spark, will render starting difficult. It may be that the plug points have become burnt, consequently widening the gap, and in this case the points should be closed. A little gauge for setting the points of the plugs and the contact points of the magneto is on the market; it only costs a few pence, and is well worth having. Failing this, do *not* use a "visiting" card as a gauge.

Sooted Plugs. If the plug is sooted or coated with a sticky black film, it should be taken to pieces (plugs with detachable centres are recommended to admit of this) and the centre cleaned with a piece of rag soaked in petrol, and the electrodes (the two points) cleaned bright with a piece of emery cloth. The body of the plug should be scraped out with a knife. The presence of a heavy carbon deposit on the plug shows that the engine is over lubricated, and the remedy here is obvious.

The Gap of the Plug Points. Sometimes, after closing the points of a plug, the rider will notice that the engine requires a

FAULTS: THEIR LOCATION AND REMEDY 131

different setting of the advance and retard lever to get the same condition of running as was obtained before the plug was adjusted. This is because the closing of the plug points is equivalent to slightly advancing the ignition. The converse is equally true; opening the points will slightly retard the ignition.

Defective Insulation of Plug. Don't forget to inspect the porcelain or mica insulation of the plug, the former may be cracked, and the latter may be " scaling," and a new centre should be purchased if this is found to be the case.

Pre-ignition. Although a plug with scaly mica insulation may appear to be sparking well outside the cylinder, the point to remember is that these " scales " become red-hot and cause pre-ignition, which means the too early firing of the charge. It may be noticed that by advancing the ignition too far a knock is caused, and pre-ignition (see Ignition Troubles) may cause a knock. A little thought will show that if the compressed charge is fired too early the gas is tending to force the piston back before it reaches the top of the stroke. When the spark is ordinarily advanced it actually does this, but beyond a certain limit a knock is heard which ceases when the ignition is retarded. The knock is probably due to the reversal of pressure on the piston head, although there are various theories to account for it. Other causes of pre-ignition are the plug points becoming red-hot, incandescence of carbon deposit or some rough part of the combustion chamber. Do not use plugs with thin electrodes (see also the note on " Pinking " later on).

Defective High-Tension Cable. It is not often that the high-tension cable may cause trouble, but sometimes, if it has been allowed to come into contact with the hot cylinder it may be found that the insulation is burnt away in one spot, allowing the bared wire to touch some part of the engine or other metallic portion and short-circuit the current. To cure this, bind the affected spot with insulating tape. Rain will sometimes cause failure of the ignition or misfiring, due to the water on the cable giving rise to a short circuit. This is comparatively rare.

Trouble with the Contact Breaker. This is not of frequent occurrence, but it must be mentioned. After running the machine for some hundreds of miles it may be found that misfiring develops at high speeds. If the plug is found to be correct, remove the cover of the magneto, rotate the engine by means of the kick-starter, and notice whether the points " make and break," or whether sparking is occurring across them. If the latter is found to be the case, it is almost certain that you will find that the points are pitted and do not make good contact, and they must be carefully trimmed with a file so that the two faces are absolutely flat. If they are not badly burnt, a strip of fine emery cloth may be doubled and pulled backwards and forwards between the points. Incidentally, if the spark across the points is large, the condenser has broken down, and this is a job which can only be put right by the makers. Whilst the cover is off, check the gap by means of the gauge already mentioned, and if incorrect, adjust them with a small spanner until the gauge just passes between them, when they are fully separated by means of the cam.

Broken Contact Spring. If you are riding and the ignition fails suddenly, it is likely that the " make and break " spring has become broken. This means that the points do not return, and quite an effective dodge to get you home is to use a rubber band to return the points.

Rocker Arm Sticking. Sometimes the rider will find that occasional misfiring, or even complete stoppage, is due to the rocker arm in the magneto being stuck. It will be noticed that this has a small bush as a bearing, and in damp weather this sometimes swells and causes the rocker to stick. The proper cure here is to remove the bush and carefully ease it with emery cloth or a file. Do *not* oil it, for even oil will cause the bush to swell.

Defective Carbon Brush. Examine the connection between the carbon brush and the cable. Beads of water or grit may be found between the contacts. It is easy to remove the carbon brush and make quite sure that the carbon is not cracked or broken.

Slipped Magneto Timing. This is caused by the slipping of the sprocket on the armature shaft, of course, causing the spark to occur at the wrong time. To check the timing open the compression tap and pass a piece of wire about 8 in. long through, so that it touches the piston. Now rotate the engine, and by the rise and fall of the piece of wire and watching the valves observe when the piston is at the top of the compression stroke, and then inspect the " make and break " to see that the points are correctly separated.

Testing Twin-cylinder Engines for Misfiring. When irregular running is experienced with a twin-cylinder machine, it is simple to find out which cylinder is misfiring. Obtain a long *wooden*

FAULTS: THEIR LOCATION AND REMEDY 133

handled screwdriver (you will get a shock if you use a metal handled one) and with the engine running, place the tip of the blade on the plug terminal and touch the cylinder with any other part of the blade; this will short-circuit the plug so that the engine is only firing on the other cylinder. By testing both cylinders in this way one may soon observe which one is wrong, or whether both are wrong.

Another method is to disconnect the lead from one plug and start the engine, testing the other cylinder in the same way.

CARBURETTOR TROUBLES

Even on the first run the rider speedily becomes aware that the carburettor is a sensitive instrument, which soon complains when it is not correctly adjusted. The levers, he finds, must be set just so for given conditions. Even at best a carburettor is an inefficient device, and a fortune awaits the inventor of one which is truly automatic, supplying the proper mixture for all engine speeds. The writer once made a device which consisted of a sort of chamber in which the gas was mixed, the engine sucking in the properly-mixed gas direct from this chamber. It was quite successful, but too expensive to make.

The rider must learn how to detect inefficient carburation, and so to control the carburettor that an efficient mixture for a given set of conditions is obtained.

The weather has an important effect on carburation. The rider will soon notice that the engine seems to run better at night or in damp weather, and this fact has led many experimenters to try " humidifying " the mixture by injecting water spray into it—with indifferent results up to the present. He will notice that by partly closing the air, opening the throttle, and slightly retarding the ignition, the engine does not seem to knock or thump on steep hills, as it may do even on bottom gear if the adjustment is not made. The author has tried in the succeeding paragraphs to anticipate almost every carburettor trouble, and to show the remedy.

" Popping Back " in the Carburettor. This is one of the commonest carburettor troubles, and usually occurs when the throttle and air are opened beyond a certain point, the effect being occasional popping or " spitting back " through the carburettor—a sort of sneezing of the engine. Gradually closing the air usually will cure it, but if " popping back " in the carburettor occurs when the machine is throttled down to ten or twelve m.p.h., it is a sign that a larger jet is necessary.

In changing a jet, it is necessary to see that the fibre washers are removed with the jet, as should one be left at the top of the hole and another jet be fitted, there would be two washers at the top and only one at the bottom, and petrol would leak in consequence. Petrol may leak from the float chamber if the jet is not thoroughly screwed into position, so that this matter should be carefully attended to.

Knocks and " Pinking " Due to Incorrect Mixture. Knocks or " pinking " in engines can be caused through wrong mixture, as well as by mechanical defects or pre-ignition (dealt with later on). Too rich or even too weak a mixture is one of the frequent causes of " pinking," a word which in itself describes the sort of knock given forth. It is an irritating sound like a tap, tap on the inside of the cylinder, and as yet no satisfactory explanation of it has been given. The generally accepted view is that the engine gets very hot owing to the use of too rich a mixture, and at a critical temperature eventually causes the charge to detonate or explode, instead of the flame caused by ignition being slowly propagated. It is, then, *overheating* which really causes " pinking," and it necessarily follows that any cause of overheating also causes pinking.

A jet should be fitted to the carburettor of such a size that full air can just be used at full throttle. A smaller jet is necessary in summer than the one used in winter.

The Petrol Level. Too low a petrol level will cause " popping back," even though the jet be of proper size, but it is wise not to alter the petrol level without good cause. If it is about $\frac{1}{32}$ in. below the top of the jet it is correct, and further adjustment, if necessary, should be made by means of the jet.

Choked Petrol Pipe, etc. Sometimes the petrol pipe will become choked with foreign matter which has found its way through the gauze placed over the tank outlet. In such a case the rider will have mysterious engine stoppages and popping back, due of course to a starved engine. He will stop to inspect, and by that time sufficient petrol has trickled by to enable the carburettor to be flooded, so that the engine starts easily, only to stop again a few yards on. When these symptoms develop, completely disconnect the petrol pipe, and by means of the tyre pump, blow it clean, and also clean out the gauze in the tank and carburettor.

Air Lock. The cause of this trouble has already been fully dealt with, and the rider will be made aware of it by symptoms similar to those already noted in the preceding paragraph. The remedies there given should be applied.

FAULTS: THEIR LOCATION AND REMEDY

Water in Petrol. This trouble is of a more serious nature, for once water has entered the carburettor it must be taken down and thoroughly wiped dry. It will cause engine stoppage, misfiring, or " popping back." It is wise to drain the tank and use the petrol for cleaning purposes, otherwise the trouble may recur. Also blow the gauzes clear.

Carburettor Flooding. Carburettor flooding is caused by (1) leaning the machine so that the float chamber is raised above the level of the jet (refer back to Fig. 45), (2) grit between the needle valve and the seating, or (3) a float that leaks and has become partly filled with petrol, preventing the needle from seating home. Overheating usually accompanies it, when the flooding takes place whilst riding. The remedy for cause (1) is obvious ; for cause (2) the union connecting the carburettor with the petrol supply should be disconnected and the petrol drained from the carburettor. This will wash the grit away.

A punctured or " petrol logged " float can usually be discovered by noting whether its needle (the " tickler ") is sluggish in action, but if it cannot be so detected, remove the float from the needle and rattle it, when the presence of petrol inside will manifest itself. A piece of sticky paper placed over the hole after the petrol has been shaken out, or even plugging the hole with a piece of soap, will effect a temporary remedy.

Air Leak. This usually takes place between the joints of the induction pipe and carburettor joints, and binding with adhesive rubber tape will speedily cure matters.

Choked Air Vent in Petrol Tank. This is a trouble which the rider may easily mistake for air lock, or choked petrol pipe. It is obvious that as petrol flows from the tank to the carburettor, air must be able to pass into the tank, and if the vent is choked a partial vacuum is formed in the tank, causing air lock. The remedy is obvious.

Damaged Carburettor Slides and Broken Cables. Any trouble with these will present itself in the form of the machine refusing satisfactorily to answer to the operation of the control levers. Sometimes a piece of grit will become lodged between the slides and their barrel, wedging one or both of them, and causing the action to be sluggish. More often than not, however, defective controls are due to frayed or broken cables, and it is wise to get them renewed at the nearest garage ; the job only takes half an hour or so.

If the throttle wire breaks whilst riding, the standard dodge is to change over the air-slide cable to the throttle, and to fix the air-slide in some suitable position, where it is considered it will enable the engine to start easily and run satisfactorily. Don't omit occasionally to oil the cables, by detaching the handle-bar end and letting oil slowly drip between the outer casing and the cable. Stretched cables, a common trouble, should of course be shortened.

TABLE I
Engine Refuses to Start

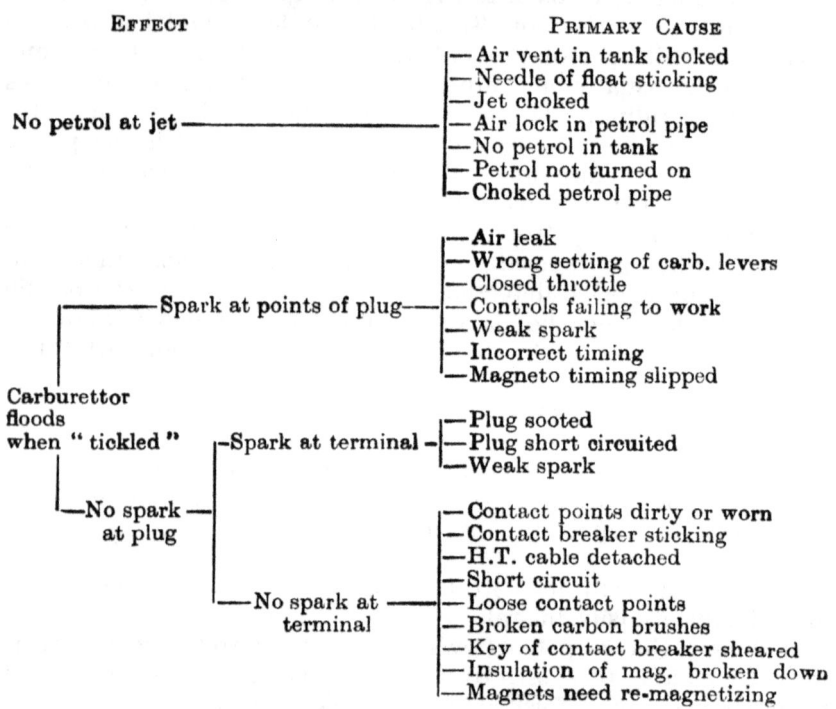

ENGINE TROUBLES

Really the troubles concerned with the engine are caused by one or a combination of the faults dealt with in connection with the carburettor and ignition, but one or two others need attention and summary here.

Starting Troubles. One of the chief problems met with in motor-cycling concerns easy starting. When the engine is fairly new and in "tune" it should start from cold without priming at the first or second kick.

In very cold weather the oil between the piston and cylinder

FAULTS: THEIR LOCATION AND REMEDY   137

becomes congealed, making it difficult to turn the engine over at an efficient starting speed ; also the gas, passing along the cold induction pipe, condenses, so that a proper mixture does not enter the cylinder.

Piston Leakage. This is caused by worn rings, rings gummed up, or uneven cylinder wear. The rings should not be allowed

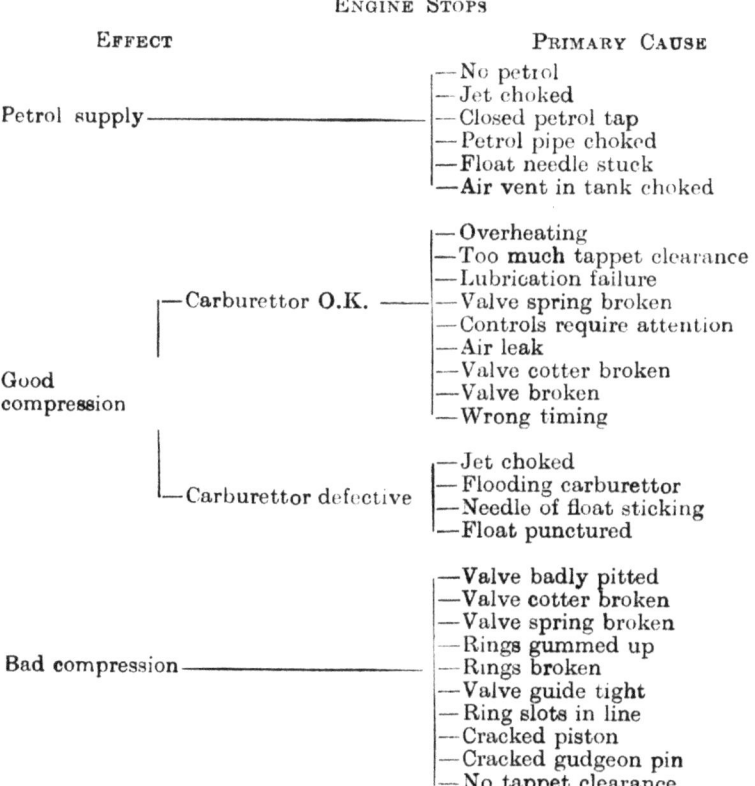

TABLE II
Engine Stops

Effect		Primary Cause
Petrol supply		—No petrol —Jet choked —Closed petrol tap —Petrol pipe choked —Float needle stuck —Air vent in tank choked
Good compression	Carburettor O.K.	—Overheating —Too much tappet clearance —Lubrication failure —Valve spring broken —Controls require attention —Air leak —Valve cotter broken —Valve broken —Wrong timing
	Carburettor defective	—Jet choked —Flooding carburettor —Needle of float sticking —Float punctured
Bad compression		—Valve badly pitted —Valve cotter broken —Valve spring broken —Rings gummed up —Rings broken —Valve guide tight —Ring slots in line —Cracked piston —Cracked gudgeon pin —No tappet clearance

to wear so that the gap is wider than $\frac{3}{64}$ in. New rings always leak until they have worn in to the cylinder. Notable loss of power accompanies piston leakage. Where three rings are fitted the gaps should be 120° apart, and when only two are provided 180° apart. When the gaps work into line, slight loss of compression may be noticed.

Leakage Round Plug and Compression Tap. If this is suspected, place some thick oil on the seating, and observe if bubbles form on the compression stroke. A new copper asbestos washer should be fitted if a leak is present.

Broken Valve. A broken valve—which, however, is a very rare occurrence—can be detected by testing the compression, or, presuming the tappets are correctly adjusted, the stem of the broken valve will be in contact with the tappet head.

Valve Bounce. Valve bounce is caused by weak springs, which should at once be replaced.

TABLE III
Engine Runs Badly

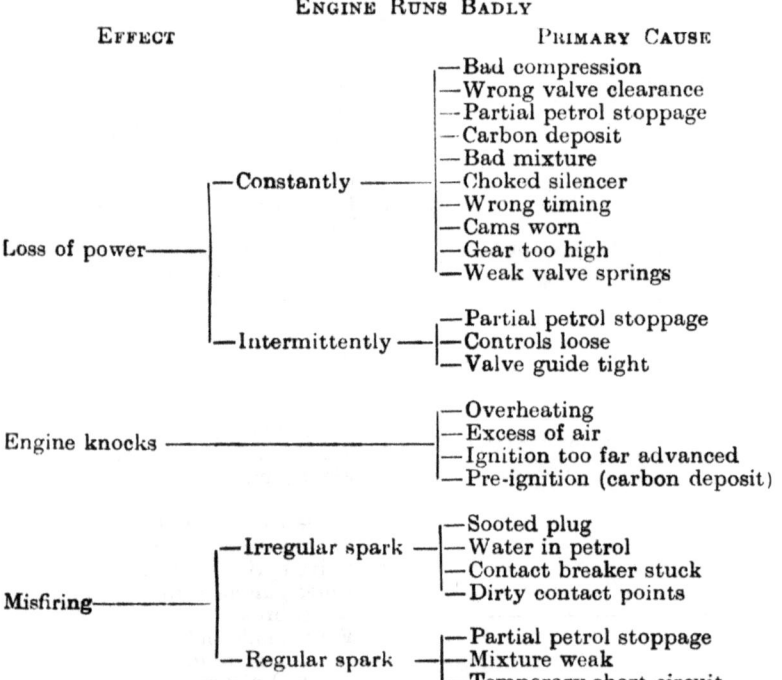

Effect		Primary Cause
Loss of power	Constantly	Bad compression Wrong valve clearance Partial petrol stoppage Carbon deposit Bad mixture Choked silencer Wrong timing Cams worn Gear too high Weak valve springs
	Intermittently	Partial petrol stoppage Controls loose Valve guide tight
Engine knocks		Overheating Excess of air Ignition too far advanced Pre-ignition (carbon deposit)
Misfiring	Irregular spark	Sooted plug Water in petrol Contact breaker stuck Dirty contact points
	Regular spark	Partial petrol stoppage Mixture weak Temporary short circuit

Valve Clearance. Check the clearance on S.V. models when the engine is hot, to allow for expansion. The clearance should be as previously recommended. An ordinary visiting card should not be used for the purpose.

Valve Sticking. Valve stem may be bent, hole in guide too small, carbon deposit in the guide, or weak spring.

The Cause of "Knocks." Every motor-cycle at some time or other develops what is commonly called "knock." It is a most elusive thing to trace, and, moreover, annoying to the rider.

FAULTS: THEIR LOCATION AND REMEDY

The knock may not, as we have already seen, always be a mechanical one, but is usually caused by one of the following items: advancing the ignition; too rich a mixture; carbon on the piston getting incandescent and pre-igniting the charge (same effect as too far advance of ignition); loose flywheel (an alarming mechanical knock as if the big ends were loose); play in the big ends or gudgeon pins; magneto sprocket loose on shaft, which also causes misfiring.

TABLE IV
Engine Stops due to Ignition

Effect		Primary Cause
No spark at plug	—No spark at magneto—	—Contact points dirty —Short circuit —Stuck contact breaker —Loose contact points —Carbon brushes broken —Key sheaved of contact breaker —Spring of contact breaker broken —Breakdown of insulation —Condenser defective
	—Spark at magneto—	—Plug sooted —Timing of magneto slipped —H.T. cable detached —Plug broken

Overheating. Usually due to too rich a mixture, load too heavy, exhaust valve not lifting to full extent, spark retarded, lack of lubrication, excessive use of low gear, gear too high.

Hot Crank Case. Due to worn piston rings or bad compression.

Colour of Exhaust. Black smoke denotes too rich a mixture; blue smoke excess of lubricating oil.

Explosions in Silencer. Due to misfiring or too rich a mixture.

Rapid Deposition of Carbon. Caused by over-lubrication, too rich a mixture, or poor quality of petrol.

CHAPTER IX

LEGAL MATTERS

The legal matters regarding licensing and registration having been disposed of in Chapter II, it remains to deal with questions anent breakage of the law—what to do and say, and what not to do and say. It is wise to remember that the legal departments of the Automobile Association and the other clubs mentioned, are always glad to advise members who may be involved in difficulties arising out of collisions or other accidents upon the road.

Requests for advice should be made immediately the accident has occurred, and not after the case has been prejudiced by letters having been written or money having been given to other parties involved in the accident.

If representation is desired at the Court, the summons should be sent as soon as served.

What to do in Case of Accident. The first thing to do in case of accident is to obtain the names and addresses of at least two witnesses who are likely to assist your case. Take down on paper careful details of the side of the road on which you were travelling, the speed, the width of the road and the condition of its surface, the signs given (whether by hand or horn, or both), whether the other vehicle (if any) carried lights, and take measurements which may be of assistance to the case, as well as the number of the vehicle and the description. The rider must, when requested, give his name and address, and produce the insurance certificate. If an injured person is likely to make a claim, an independent medical man should be called to examine him and issue a report. Do not engage in correspondence without legal advice, or if this is not taken, make clear that all your statements in the letter are made without prejudice to your case; and refrain from making statements, either at the time of the accident or afterwards, which might be construed as an admission of liability. Do not offer money to the injured party, for motives of sympathy may be misconstrued into an admission of legal liability. If a policeman is not available, all accidents must be reported at the nearest police station with twenty-four hours.

The Order to Stop. A person in charge of a horse may order a motor-cyclist to stop, and so may a constable in uniform, or a person injured by your machine. Apart from this, it is inadvisable to stop when asked to do so by others. The sign to stop should be made as already noted in the chapter on Driving. Any pedestrian may order a motor-cyclist to stop.

LEGAL MATTERS

Furious Driving. A person driving furiously renders himself liable to conviction for the following offences—

(1) Driving to common danger.
(2) If anyone injured, indictment for causing bodily harm.
(3) If anyone killed, indictment for manslaughter.
(4) To arrest by any person, whether constable or not, who sees offence committed.

Driving Licence. The driving licence must be *signed by the owner*.

Refusing Address. To anyone who complains that the motorist has committed an offence of driving to the common danger, the driver must give his name and address. If the driver refuses, or gives a false name and address, he is liable to fine not exceeding £20 for a first offence, and to heavier penalties for a second or subsequent offence. He may be arrested without warrant by a constable who saw the alleged offence committed, whether the constable is in uniform or not. The owner, if required, must give all the information in his power which may lead to the identification of the driver, and if he does not do so is himself liable to the same penalty as the driver.

Warning of Approach. It is compulsory to give audible warning of approach whenever it is necessary. Failure to do so renders the driver liable to conviction for driving to the common danger, and to an action for negligence if injury is caused as a result of such neglect.

Exhaust Cut-out. It is illegal to use an exhaust cut-out, or any device which enables the exhaust to escape without first passing through the silencer.

Arrest. The driver is liable to arrest by a police constable (whether in uniform or not) if he refuses his name and address, refuses to produce his licence on demand, if his machine does not bear the identification (registration) mark, or, if he is suspected of being under the influence of drink or drugs.

Illumination. (See also Chapter II.) Motor-cycles with sidecars attached must carry on the latter a white light forward and red light to rear. The driver must have the identification plate illuminated half an hour after sunset and half an hour before sunrise (extended by one hour during Summer Time). Solo motor-cycles must also carry a red rear light.

Rules Regarding Number Plate. The driver of a motor-cycle is guilty of an offence if the number plate is not properly fixed, or if it is in any way obscured or rendered not easily distinguishable or not properly illuminated, unless he can prove that he has taken reasonable steps to prevent this, and if the driver is not the owner the latter may be guilty of aiding and abetting.

Regarding the Registration Book. When a licence is issued a Registration Book is handed to the owner, and this must be sent to the Council with whom the vehicle is registered, or
(1) When any alteration is made to the vehicle.
(2) On sale or other change of ownership.
(3) On change of address
(4) When vehicle broken up, destroyed, or sent permanently out of the United Kingdom (see paragraph in the chapter on " Buying and Selling a Second-hand Machine ").

Obstruction. A motor-cycle must not be left for an unreasonable or unnecessary time on the highway.

Right of Appeal. A person convicted of any offence under the Road Traffic Act, 1930, has the right of appeal to the next Court of General Quarter Sessions. A right of appeal lies against an order disqualifying any person from holding or obtaining a driver's licence.

Speed Limit. According to the strict letter of the law, the speed in public parks must not exceed 20 miles per hour. Special limits of 8 or 10 miles per hour are fixed in certain towns and villages. These must be strictly observed. The new speed limit of 30 m.p.h. applies only to built-up areas (a built-up area is one in which lamp-posts are erected not more than 200 yards apart).

Time Allowed for Production of Driving Licence. If the rider cannot produce his driving licence when asked by a police officer, he will not be guilty of an offence provided that he produces it within five days at any police station he nominates.

Insurance Certificate. The insurance certificate must be carried by the driver and produced upon the request of the police.

Automatic Traffic Signals. It has just been decided, as the result of a test case, that these signals tell you when to stop, not where to stop. The lines marked across the road at points where automatic traffic signals are used show the stopping line.

Hire Purchase. When motor-cycles are bought on the hire purchase system, the following facts should be borne in mind.

Nearly all motor-cycle agents take advantage of arrangements offered by special hire purchase corporations. By this method their hire purchase business becomes ordinary cash sales, the corporation buying the machine from the dealer and letting on hire purchase agreement to his customer. From that time the responsibility for the collection of the monthly instalments is taken over by the corporation. The machine does not become the property of the hirer until the last instalment has been paid. Under most hire purchase agreements the hirer undertakes to pay deposit and the insurance premium on signing the agreement; to pay the monthly instalment on the due dates, to keep the motor-cycle in good repair and to pay all licence duties, not to use the machine contrary to the law, and not to jeopardize the owner's (that is the finance corporation) right of ownership. The corporation may collect the motor-cycle and dispose of it for a reasonable price if the hirer defaults in payment of the monthly instalments. If there is a surplus this is returnable to the hirer and a deficiency must be met by the hirer. These are the usual terms applying to hire purchase. They may not apply to hire purchase systems run by B.S.A. agents, but annoyance can be avoided if the hire purchase agreement is thoroughly studied before being signed.

CHAPTER X

BUYING AND SELLING AN OLD MOUNT

Buying a Second-hand Machine. The purchase of a second-hand machine is one which should be carefully approached by the inexperienced, for so many machines with serious engine troubles which outwardly appear to be in excellent condition are available that it is difficult to detect fakes, especially when skilfully executed. Only the most reputable makes should be purchased, for one may then be reasonably assured of being able to obtain spares. A skilled motor-cyclist where possible should accompany the inexperienced. The very efficient B.S.A. spares service enables spare parts for any particular B.S.A. model, however old, to be obtained within a few hours. It is always wise to purchase a second-hand machine from a reputable agent.

Year of Make. First ascertain the year of make (this may be verified by reference to the registration book) by noting the engine and frame numbers. A list of engine and frame numbers of B.S.A. machines from 1914 onwards can be obtained from the manufacturers.

Examining the Machine. First examine the frame for cracks, and to see that it is true. Next look to the condition of the tools and accessories, and test the head and front forks for play. The tyres and wheel bearings should not be missed, and the points of attachment need viewing if a sidecar is fitted. Having satisfied oneself that in general the machine is in reasonable condition, proceed to test the engine. The condition of the nuts is a good index as to whether the machine has needed frequent adjustment.

Testing the Engine. Firstly, turn the engine over slowly by means of the kick-starter and see that the compression is good. Next rotate it and listen for knocks indicative of wear. Perhaps greatest wear will be detected in the valves and valve gear, but these parts are easily and cheaply replaced. If the valves have been repeatedly ground-in this fact will readily be apparent (refer back to Fig. 83), for the valve seats will be relatively wide and deep sunk, and is an index of careless use or old age—a fact which should temper one's views of the other parts. The valve-gear mechanism should be exposed and the wheels and cams carefully examined. If worn they will require renewal.

The condition of the piston and cylinder can only be gauged by experience, but if wear is detected (piston will " slap " in the cylinder when the engine is running) an allowance might be asked. It must be pointed out that a piston which slaps in its cylinder should not be regarded as a minor defect—it usually is indicative of an oval cylinder, necessitating regrinding of the cylinder and a new (oversize) piston, and it is wise not to make a purchase. There is an exception in the case of an alloy piston. This is a fairly loose fit in the cylinder when cold.

The Trial Run. After the preliminary inspection, the engine should be started and attention devoted to noise caused by worn cams and timing gears, worn piston or cylinder, or other engine noises. A trial run should in all cases be insisted on, so that one may be satisfied as to the control and general running. The trial run can easily be arranged with a combination, for the owner, if dubious, can accompany the prospective purchaser in the sidecar. If a solo machine, the owner can reasonably expect a deposit as a token of good faith before allowing the intending purchaser to take a trial run. If satisfied that the machine is in good condition, bargain for a reduction in price, for most owners ask for more than they expect to get for the machine. Second-hand prices may be ascertained by reference to the weekly motor-cycle papers.

A Warning. The reader is advised to make quite sure that the vendor is the real owner of the machine, for if he purchases and the machine is subsequently claimed by the real owner, he must return the machine to the rightful owner and has no redress except the doubtful one of suing the vendor if he can be found. Carefully inspect the registration book and check the name and address.

Selling a Second-hand Mount. The foregoing information indicates in some measure the questions likely to be asked, and before taking steps to dispose of the machine it should be placed in reasonable selling condition. As such it will avoid irritating correspondence after sale, and will command a higher price than if the defects are left unremedied ; as well, excuses have not to be raised when the defects are discovered by the purchaser.

Selling Through an Agency. Several firms undertake to sell second-hand machines, the procedure in most cases being to value the machine and to allow the agent a commission on that price. As, however, such agents usually sell the machine at a higher price than the owner's figure, it follows that too high a value renders the machine of little service to the agent.

Part Exchange. When the purchase of a new machine is contemplated, best value for the old one can be obtained by a part exchange transaction.

Selling by Advertising in Trade Papers. This is usually an excellent method of selling, because the trade papers classify the machines, so that an intending purchaser of a B.S.A. has only to look down the small advertisement columns of one of the motor cycling papers to see comparative prices.

Advertising in the daily and local press is also an excellent method of selling.

The reader is reminded of the rules given in Chapter II (regarding the registration book) which apply when the machine changes hands. Post Card Form No. R.F. 70 must be filled in and posted by the vendor of a second-hand motor-cycle. It is obtainable at all post offices. Do not let the machine change hands until the purchase price is handed over.

Checking the Age of a Second-hand Machine. If an intending purchaser is in doubt as to the exact age of a machine, he can check it by means of the engine and frame numbers. These cannot, however, be taken as an absolutely definite guide; they are simply works numbers.

The reader will readily appreciate that if there is no material change in design in a certain model from one season to another, that model ceases to belong in particular to the expired season, and since the maker's guarantee dates from the sale of the machine by the agent to the customer, and not its delivery from the works, frame and engine numbers are a rough guide only; they are, however, essential for identification when ordering replacements of any description.

CHAPTER XI

THE 1936 MODELS

For the 1936 season several new models of outstanding importance are offered, and conspicuous amongst these are the two "Empire Star" models of 348 c.c. and 496 c.c. capacity respectively. These machines, which are identical in design, except for the difference in engine capacity, possess several novel features, which are the subject of special notes below.

The lightweight range is enhanced by the inclusion of a new 2·49 h.p. O.H.V. Light de Luxe model, which follows in general design the popular 2·49 h.p. O.H.V. Standard model, but which has a new four-speed gearbox, improved front fork assembly, and other features detailed below.

The heavy group of machines has been considerably modified for 1936. The 5·95 h.p. type is represented by a side valve model only, which now appears as an upright engine mounted in a new frame. The new 5.95 h.p. side valve engine has been designed as a robust and powerful unit capable of propelling heavy loads at moderately high speeds, and possessing power output characteristics which are reflected in its remarkable flexibility at low speeds. Its top gear performance is in fact astounding.

The power unit fitted to the 1936 9·86 h.p. Twin is practically unchanged, no modifications of a serious nature having been found necessary, but it is now housed in a new frame of immense strength.

An entirely new model of unique interest is included in the 1936 heavy group. This is a 750 c.c. O.H.V. Vee-Twin with dry-sump lubrication. In design the engine follows to a certain extent the now well-known B.S.A. 4·98 O.H.V. Twin.

For solo work the new 750 c.c. Twin provides an entirely new thrill, for the machine is neither excessively heavy nor difficult to handle.

During the 1935 season the 3·48 h.p. O.H.V. de Luxe model has acquired a first-class reputation as a Trials Machine. In view of this, it has been decided to list a special version of this model for 1936 with competition equipment.

The other members of the B.S.A. range of motor cycles for 1936 are based on the 1935 models, but in every case important improvements are incorporated. These are detailed against the various models to which they apply in the specifications, and in the following notes these improvements are described.

Improved Lubrication Systems. Amongst the most important of the modifications to the 1936 models is the improved lubrication system fitted to the middle group machine having the integral sump. The capacity of the sump has now been increased to a full half gallon. This has the dual result of ensuring a lower oil temperature under running conditions and a greater mileage before replenishment in cases of emergency.

In addition to the increased oil capacity the pump has been modified to give a higher rate of delivery, and the oil supply to the big-end is controlled quite automatically.

The dry sump lubrication systems fitted to 2·49 h.p. O.H.V. de Luxe, 3·48 h.p. O.H.V. de Luxe, 4·98 h.p. Twin and the new 7·48 Twin are similarly modified, except that there has been no need to increase the size of the separate oil tanks.

Modified Pistons. For certain of the higher duty 1936 pistons a new low expansion alloy is used, which possesses obvious advantages under special temperature conditions, and all pistons are now fitted with slotted scraper rings of high efficiency. The function of these is to permit of a much greater rate of oil circulation throughout the engine, without any increase in oil consumption.

It will be realized that the combined effect of the modification to the lubrication systems and pistons is of great importance to the user, since not only is cylinder and general engine wear greatly retarded, but engine efficiency and silence are considerably enhanced.

Constant Wheelbase Front Forks. It will be remembered that last season constant wheelbase action was applied to certain models. This has become so popular a feature that it is now extended to the remaining solo members of the range. This action is arranged by means of a special linkage, which ensures that within the range of front fork deflection the wheelbase of the machine is unaltered. On rough surfaces at speed, consequently, the maximum possible degree of stability is obtained.

The Empire Star Models. This model, which is listed in two sizes, has been introduced to supply the demand for a de luxe sporting mount, attractive in appearance, possessing refinements of a really comprehensive character, and designed for ultra-reliability coupled with a sparkling performance.

The specification of the 348 c.c. engine has been developed from that of the well-known 3·48 h.p. O.H.V. Special, which acquired an excellent sports reputation, while the 500 c.c. size, has been redesigned on a thoroughly practical yet scientific

THE 1936 MODELS

basis, which has ensured the correct co-relation of bore-stroke ratio, port design, valve displacement and compression ratio, so that the resultant engine possesses extreme flexibility, complete freedom from detonation, and an outstanding performance. Coupled with these dynamic engine characteristics are the inclusion in the specification of a new crankcase of great strength, larger mainshaft with double roller bearings, reinforced flywheels, a large B.S.A. multi-plate dry clutch with special fabric linings and operating in a genuine oil-bath primary transmission, oil feed to the rear chain, an entirely new impervious finish to the crankcase and gearbox, a new low-expansion alloy piston, and a hardened and tempered alloy cylinder barrel of extreme durability. The adoption of this new cylinder material marks an important new stage in the history of automobile engineering, and it represents the successful completion of a programme of research extending over a period of years.

ANALYSIS OF THE 1936 B.S.A. RANGE

In addition to the principal new features above there are many new items included in the specification, but as these call for no special description they are included in the following analysis without further comment.

1·49 h.p. O.H.V. Model X-0. As 1935 Model X35-0, but with slotted scraper piston ring, permitting greater oil circulation without increased consumption; constant wheelbase front forks; new horn mounting in front of cylinder; and improved clutch.

2·49 h.p. S.V. Model C-1. As 1935 Model B35-1, but with slotted scraper piston ring, permitting greater oil circulation without increased consumption; constant wheelbase front forks; Lucas Magdyno equipment; electric horn mounted in front angle of frame to give more compact assembly; quick release petrol filler cap; new front mudguard; new Terry saddle; and improved clutch.

2·49 h.p. O.H.V. Model B-2. As 1935 Model B35-2, but with slotted scraper piston ring, permitting greater oil circulation without increased consumption; constant wheelbase front forks; Lucas Magdyno equipment; quick release petrol filler cap; new front mudguard; new horn mounting in front of cylinder; new Terry saddle; and multiple clutch.

2·49 h.p. O.H.V. Light De Luxe, Model B-18. As 1935 Model B35-2, but with slotted scraper piston rings, permitting greater oil circulation without increased consumption; Lucas Magdyno equipment; front forks and handlebar as Model R4; steering damper; stronger back stays; new four-speed gearbox with multiple clutch; oil tank under saddle; new petrol tank; quick release petrol filler cap; 3·25 × 19 tyres; Terry adjustable saddle twin toolbox as 1935 Model R35-5; and unswept exhaust pipe extra.

2·49 h.p. O.H.V. De Luxe Model B-3. As 1935 Model B35-3, but with slotted scraper piston ring, permitting greater oil circulation without increased consumption; quick release petrol filler cap; new knee grip; new front mudguard and number plate fixing; constant wheelbase front forks; Terry adjustable saddle; new shape exhaust pipe; improved lubrication system; and foot gear-change standard.

3·48 h.p. O.H.V. De Luxe Model R-4. As 1935 Model R35-4, but with slotted scraper piston ring, permitting of greater oil circulation without increased consumption; quick release petrol filler cap; new knee grip; new front mudguard and number plate fixing; constant wheelbase front forks; Terry adjustable saddle; new shape exhaust pipe; improved lubrication system; and foot gear-change standard.

3·48 h.p. O.H.V. De Luxe, Model R-19 (Competition Model). As 1935 Model R35-4, but with slotted scraper piston ring, permitting greater oil circulation without increased consumption; improved lubrication system; unswept exhaust pipe; specially tested engine with high compression piston; quick release petrol filler cap; constant wheelbase front forks; Dunlop saddle; chromium-plated wheels including prominent parts of hubs and brakes; chromium-plated trials mudguards; foot gear-change; spare low compression piston supplied to kit. Competition tyres—2·75-21 front, 4·00-19 rear.

3·48 h.p. O.H.V. Single Port, Model R-17. As 1935 Model R35-17, but with slotted scraper piston ring, permitting greater oil circulation without increased consumption; single port cylinder head; increased sump capacity and improved lubrication system; new petrol tank; quick release petrol filler cap; new knee grips; and new adjustable saddle.

3·48 h.p. O.H.V. "Blue Star," Model R-20. As 1935 Model R35-5, but with slotted scraper piston ring, permitting greater oil circulation without increased consumption; increased sump capacity and improved lubrication system; new petrol tank;

THE 1936 MODELS

quick release petrol filler cap; new knee grips; and new adjustable saddle.

3·48 h.p. O.H.V. "Empire Star," Model R35-5. Similar in specification to Model R35-4, except for special engine; larger diameter drive shaft, with twin bearings; hardened alloy cast iron cylinder barrel; hardened piston rings; stiffer flywheel assembly; increased sump capacity and improved lubrication system; slotted scraper piston ring, permitting greater oil circulation without increased consumption; new petrol tank with special colour scheme; special finish to petrol filler cap; new knee grips; new oil bath aluminium chaincase; new adjustable saddle; and spare piston giving alternative compression ratio.

4·99 h.p. S.V. Model W-6. As 1935 Model W35-6, but with slotted scraper piston ring, permitting greater oil circulation without increased consumption; stiffer flywheel assembly; increased sump capacity and improved lubrication system; new petrol tank; quick release petrol filler cap; quickly detachable rear wheel; new knee grips; and new adjustable saddle.

4·96 h.p. O.H.V. Model Q-7. As 1935 Model W35-7, but with bore and stroke 82 × 94 mm. (496 c.c.); stiffer flywheel assembly; slotted scraper piston ring, permitting greater oil circulation without increased consumption; increased sump capacity and improved lubrication system; new petrol tank; quick release petrol filler cap; new knee grips; new adjustable saddle.

4·96 h.p. O.H.V. "Blue Star," Model Q-21. As 1935 Model W35-8, but with bore and stroke 82 × 94 mm. (496 c.c.); stiffer flywheel assembly; slotted scraper piston ring, permitting greater oil circulation without increased consumption; increased sump capacity and improved lubrication system; new petrol tank; quick release petrol filler cap; new knee grips; and new adjustable saddle.

4·96 h.p. O.H.V. "Empire Star," Model Q-8. Similar in specification to Model W35-8 except for special engine; 82 × 94 mm. (496 c.c.); larger diameter drive shaft with twin bearings; stiffer flywheel assembly; hardened alloy cast iron cylinder barrel; hardened piston rings; increased sump capacity and improved lubrication system; slotted scraper piston ring, permitting greater oil circulation without increased consumption; new petrol tank with special colour scheme; special finish to various parts; quick release petrol filler cap; new knee grips; new oil bath aluminium chain case; new adjustable saddle; and spare piston giving alternative compression ratio.

4·98 h.p. O.H.V. Twin, Model J-12. As 1935 Model J35-12, but with improved lubrication system; quick release filler cap; slotted scraper piston ring, permitting greater oil circulation without increased consumption.

5·95 h.p. S.V. Model M-10. Replaces 1935 Model M35-10. As 1935 Model W35-6, but with stroke increased to 105 mm. giving a capacity of 595 c.c.; increased sump capacity and improved lubrication system; slotted scraper piston ring, permitting greater oil circulation without increased consumption; larger diameter drive shaft; twin drive shaft bearings; new petrol tank; quick release petrol filler cap; new quickly detachable and interchangeable wheels; new knee grips; adjustable saddle; new duplex cradle from with forged steel backbone; new forks of great strength with constant wheelbase action; 4.00 × 18 tyres.

7·48 h.p. O.H.V. Twin Model Y-12. An entirely new 750 c.c. O.H.V. Vee Twin. Bore and stroke 71 × 94½ (748 c.c. capacity); slotted scraper piston ring, permitting greater oil circulation without increased consumption; dry sump lubrication with oil tank (half gallon) under saddle; large diameter drive shaft with twin bearings; articulated big-end bearings; new duplex cradle frame with forged steel backbone; new forks of great strength, with constant wheelbase action; large capacity petrol tank (3¾ gallons); quick release petrol filler cap; new quickly detachable and interchangeable wheels; 4·00 × 18 tyres; four-speed gearbox; and adjustable saddle.

9·86 h.p. S.V. Twin, Model G-14. As 1936 Model Y-13, but with engine as 1935 G35-14; slotted scraper piston ring, permitting greater oil circulation without increased consumption; modified exhaust system.

USEFUL INFORMATION

TABLE OF GRADIENTS

Gradient.	Per Cent.	No. of Feet Rise or Fall in 1 Mile.
1 in 5	20	1,056
1 ,, 6	17	880
1 ,, 7	14	754
1 ,, 8	12½	660
1 ,, 9	11	587
1 ,, 10	10	528
1 ,, 11	9	480
1 ,, 12	8	440
1 ,, 13	7¾	406
1 ,, 14	7	377
1 ,, 15	6½	352
1 ,, 16	6¼	330
1 ,, 17	6	311
1 ,, 18	5½	293
1 ,, 19	5	278
1 ,, 20	5	264
1 ,, 25	4	211
1 ,, 30	3·3	176
1 ,, 35	2·8	154
1 ,, 40	2½	132

EQUIVALENT SPEEDS

Speed in M.P.H.	Time Taken to Cover 1 Mile.
10	6 minutes
15	4 ,,
20	3 ,,
25	2 ,, 24 seconds
30	2 ,,
35	1 minute 42⁶⁄₇ ,,
40	1 ,, 30 ,,
50	1 ,, 12 ,,
60	1 ,,

APPROXIMATE ENGINE REVOLUTIONS
At Different Speeds—Miles Per Hour

Gear Ratio.	4	4¼	4½	4¾	5	5¼	5½	5¾	6	6¼	6½	6¾	7
Speed in Miles Hour.													
5	260	276	292	309	325	346	358	374	388	404	420	437	453
10	520	552	584	618	650	692	716	748	775	808	840	875	905
15	780	828	876	927	975	1038	1074	1122	1160	1210	1260	1310	1360
20	1040	1104	1168	1236	1300	1384	1432	1496	1550	1615	1680	1750	1810
25	1300	1380	1460	1545	1625	1730	1790	1870	1940	2020	2100	2180	2265
30	1560	1656	1752	1854	1950	2076	2148	2244	2320	2420	2520	2620	2720
35	1820	1932	2044	2163	2275	2422	2506	2618	2710	2830	2950	3060	3170
40	2080	2208	2336	2472	2600	2768	2864	2992	3100	3230	3370	3490	3620
45	2340	2484	2628	2781	2925	3114	3222	3366	3490	3640	3790	3940	4070
50	2600	2760	2920	3090	3250	3460	3580	3740	3880	4040	4310	4370	4530
55	2860	3036	3212	3399	3575	3806	3938	4114	4270	4440	4630	4800	4980
60	3120	3312	3504	3709	3900	4152	4296	4488	4650	4850	5040	5240	5440

Diameter of Driving Wheels, 26 in. For 28 in. Wheels, multiply by 0·93.
For 24 in. Wheels, multiply revolutions by 1·08.

USEFUL INFORMATION

CYLINDER BORES AND STROKES IN MILLIMETRES AND INCHES

An Approximate Guide for Comparison

A Cylinder Measuring—	Is Equal to—
Millimetres	Inches
60 × 61½	= 2⅜ × 2$\frac{7}{16}$
63 × 80	= 2½ × 3⅛
72 × 85½	= 2$\frac{13}{16}$ × 3⅜
76 × 85	= 3 × 3$\frac{5}{16}$
80 × 98	= 3⅛ × 3⅞
85 × 98	= 3$\frac{5}{16}$ × 3⅞
90 × 90	= 3$\frac{9}{16}$ × 3$\frac{9}{16}$
90 × 110	= 3$\frac{9}{16}$ × 4$\frac{5}{16}$
95 × 115	= 3¾ × 4$\frac{9}{16}$
100 × 115	= 3$\frac{15}{16}$ × 4$\frac{9}{16}$
105 × 118	= 4⅛ × 4⅝
108 × 120	= 4¼ × 4¾
110 × 125	= 4$\frac{5}{16}$ × 4$\frac{15}{16}$
112 × 128	= 4$\frac{7}{16}$ × 5$\frac{1}{16}$
114 × 130	= 4½ × 5⅛
116 × 134	= 4$\frac{9}{16}$ × 5$\frac{5}{16}$
118 × 138	= 4⅝ × 5$\frac{7}{16}$
120 × 140	= 4¾ × 5½
122 × 143	= 4$\frac{13}{16}$ × 5⅝
124 × 146	= 4⅞ × 5¾
126 × 148	= 4$\frac{15}{16}$ × 5$\frac{13}{16}$
128 × 150	= 5$\frac{1}{16}$ × 5$\frac{15}{16}$

FORMULAE FOR H.P.

S = Stroke in centimetres
D = Diameter of cylinder in centimetres
R = Revolutions per minute
N = Number of cylinders

$$\text{R.A.C. Formula H.P.} = \frac{D^2 \times N}{16 \cdot 13}$$

A.C.U. Formula = 100 c.c. = 1 h p.

A more accurate formula is the Dendy Marshall in which—

$$\text{H.P.} = \frac{D^2 \times S \times N \times R}{200{,}000}$$

TYRE SIZE EQUIVALENTS

65 Millimetres = 2½ in.		650 Millimetres = 26 in.	
80 ,, = 3 ,,		700 ,, = 28 ,,	
85 ,, = 3¼ ,,		750 ,, = 30 ,,	
90 ,, = 3½ ,,		800 ,, = 32 ,,	
100 ,, = 4 ,,		870 ,, = 34 ,,	
105 ,, = 4¼ ,,		910 ,, = 36 ,,	
120 ,, = 5 ,,		1010 ,, = 40 ,,	

INDEX

ABROAD, taking machine, 127
Acceleration, 39
Adjusting magneto chain, 105
Adjustment of rockers, 96
Air lock, 134
Alignment of sidecar, 113

BRAKES, 42, 109, 120
Buying and selling, 144

CARBURETTOR, 62, 133
Chains, care of, 106
Cleaning the machine, 111
Clutch, 81, 110
Contact breaker, 60
Cush drive, 71

DECARBONIZING, 101
Dismantling, 80
Driving, 35
―― a combination, 44
―― in traffic, 52
―― licence, 23
Dress, 123

ENGINE decarbonization, 101
――, how it works, 56
―― revolutions, 154
―― troubles, 136

FAULTS, 130
Forks, front, 89
Four-stroke engine, principles of, 56

GRADIENTS table, 153
Grease gun lubrication, 93

HANDLEBAR fitting, 90
Highway code, 46
Hub adjustment, 117, 120

IGNITION troubles, 130
Insurance, 33

LEGAL matters, 140
Licence, driving, 23

Lubrication of rockers, 97
―― system, 82
Lubricating the engine, 35
―― the gears, 79
Luggage, 126

MAGNETO chain, adjusting, 105
――, elements of, 58
Mechanical details of B.S.A., 67
Models, various, 1, 147

NIGHT riding, 54
Number plates, 31

OIL mist lubrication, 97
Overhauling, 94

PILLION riding, 45
Piston leakage, 137
―― ring gaps, 122
Procedure on hills, 45

REASSEMBLING, 80
Re-enamelling, 116
Registration, 24
Rocker arm sticking, 132
Rules of the road, 47
Running-in, 42

SHOCK absorbers, 116
Sidecar alignment, 113
Sidecars, 19
Signals, 47
Slipped magneto timing, 132

TAPPET clearances, 95
Timing gear, 90
Touring, 123
Tyres, concerning, 43

VALVE clearances, 95
―― timing, 104

WATER in petrol, 135

AUTOBOOKS WORKSHOP MANUALS

ALFA ROMEO GIULIA 1300, 1600, 1750, 2000 1962-1978 WSM
BMW 1600 1966-1973 WSM
BMW 2500, 2800, 3.0 & 3.3 1968-1977 WSM
BMW 316, 320, 320i 1975-1977 WSM
BMW 518, 520, 520i 1973-1981 WSM
FIAT 1100, 1100D, 1100R & 1200 1957-1969 WSM
FIAT 124 1966-1974 WSM
FIAT 124 SPORT 1966-1975 WSM
FIAT 125 & 125 SPECIAL 1967-1973 WSM
FIAT 126, 126L, 126 DV, 126/650 & 126/650 DV 1972-1982 WSM
FIAT 127 SALOON, SPECIAL & SPORT, 900, 1050 1971-1981 WSM
FIAT 128 1969-1982 WSM
FIAT 1300, 1500 1961-1967 WSM
FIAT 131 MIRAFIORI 1975-1982 WSM
FIAT 132 1972-1982 WSM
FIAT 500 1957-1973 WSM
FIAT 600, 600D & MULTIPLA 1955-1969 WSM
FIAT 850 1964-1972 WSM
JAGUAR MK 1, 2 1955-1969 WSM
JAGUAR S TYPE, 420 1963-1968 WSM
JAGUAR XK 120, 140, 150 MK 7, 8, 9 1948-1961 WSM
LAND ROVER 1, 2 1948-1961 WSM
MERCEDES-BENZ 190 1959-1968 WSM
MERCEDES-BENZ 220/8 1968-1977 WSM
MERCEDES-BENZ 220B 1959-1965 WSM
MERCEDES-BENZ 230 1963-1968 WSM
MERCEDES-BENZ 250 1968-1972 WSM
MERCEDES-BENZ 280 1968-1972 WSM
MINI 1959-1980 WSM
MORRIS MINOR 1952-1971 WSM
PEUGEOT 404 1960-1975 WSM
PORSCHE 911 1964-1973 WSM
PORSCHE 911 1970-1977 WSM
RENAULT 16 1965-1979 WSM
RENAULT 8, 10, 1100 1962-1971 WSM
ROVER 3500, 3500S 1968-1976 WSM
SUNBEAM RAPIER, ALPINE 1955-1965 WSM
TRIUMPH SPITFIRE, GT6, VITESSE 1962-1968 WSM
TRIUMPH TR4, TR4A 1961-1967 WSM
VOLKSWAGEN BEETLE 1968-1977 WSM

VELOCEPRESS AUTOMOBILE BOOKS & MANUALS

ABARTH BUYERS GUIDE
AUSTIN-HEALEY 6-CYLINDER WSM
AUSTIN-HEALEY SPRITE & MG MIDGET 1958-1971 WSM
BMW 600 LIMOUSINE FACTORY WSM
BMW 600 LIMOUSINE OWNERS HAND BOOK & SERVICE MANUAL
BMW 2000 & 2002 1966-1976 WSM
BMW ISETTA FACTORY WSM
CARRERA PANAMERICANA - MEXICAN ROAD RACE (BOOK OF)
COMPLETE CATALOG OF JAPANESE MOTOR VEHICLES
CORVAIR 1960-1969 OWNERS WORKSHOP MANUAL
CORVETTE V8 1955-1962 OWNERS WORKSHOP MANUAL
DIALED IN - THE JAN OPPERMAN STORY
FERRARI 250/GT SERVICE AND MAINTENANCE
FERRARI 308 SERIES BUYER'S AND OWNER'S GUIDE
FERRARI BERLINETTA LUSSO
FERRARI BROCHURES AND SALES LITERATURE 1946-1967
FERRARI BROCHURES AND SALES LITERATURE 1968-1989
FERRARI GUIDE TO PERFORMANCE
FERRARI OPP, MAINTENANCE & SERVICE H/BOOKS 1948-1963
FERRARI OWNER'S HANDBOOK
FERRARI SERIAL NUMBERS PART I - ODD NUMBERS TO 21399
FERRARI SERIAL NUMBERS PART II - EVEN NUMBERS TO 1050
FERRARI SPYDER CALIFORNIA
FERRARI TUNING TIPS & MAINTENANCE TECHNIQUES
HENRY'S FABULOUS MODEL "A" FORD
HOW TO BUILD A FIBERGLASS CAR
HOW TO BUILD A RACING CAR
HOW TO RESTORE THE MODEL 'A' FORD
IF HEMINGWAY HAD WRITTEN A RACING NOVEL
JAGUAR E-TYPE 3.8 & 4.2 WSM
LE MANS 24 (THE BOOK THAT THE FILM WAS BASED ON)
MASERATI BROCHURES AND SALES LITERATURE
MASERATI OWNER'S HANDBOOK
METROPOLITAN FACTORY WSM
MGA & MGB OWNERS HANDBOOK & WSM
MG MIDGET TC, TD, TF & TF1500 WORKSHOP MANUAL
OBERT'S FIAT GUIDE
PERFORMANCE TUNING THE SUNBEAM TIGER
PORSCHE 356 1948-1965 WSM
PORSCHE 912 WSM
SOUPING THE VOLKSWAGEN
SOLEX CARBURETORS (EMPHASIS ON UK & EU AUTOMOBILES)
SU CARBURETORS (EMPHASIS ON UK AUTOMOBILES)
TRIUMPH TR2, TR3, TR4 1953-1965 WSM
TUNING FOR SPEED (P.E. IRVING)
VEDA ORR'S NEW REVISED HOT ROD PICTORIAL
VOLKSWAGEN TRANSPORTER, TRUCKS, STATION WAGONS WSM
VOLVO 1944-1968 ALL MODELS WSM
WEBER CARBURETORS (EMPHASIS ON ALFA & FIAT)

VELOCEPRESS THREE WHEELER BOOKS & MANUALS

BSA THREE WHEELER (BOOK OF)

BROOKLANDS BOOKS & ROAD TEST PORTFOLIOS (RTP)

AC CARS 1904-2009
ALFA ROMEO 1920-1933 ROAD TEST PORTFOLIO
ALFA ROMEO 1934-1940 ROAD TEST PORTFOLIO
BRABHAM RALT HONDA THE RON TAURANAC STORY
BUGATTI TYPE 10 TO TYPE 40 ROAD TEST PORTFOLIO
BUGATTI TYPE 10 TO TYPE 251 ROAD TEST PORTFOLIO
BUGATTI TYPE 41 TO TYPE 55 ROAD TEST PORTFOLIO
BUGATTI TYPE 57 TO TYPE 251 ROAD TEST PORTFOLIO
DELAHAYE ROAD TEST PORTFOLIO
FERRARI ROAD CARS 1946-1956 ROAD TEST PORTFOLIO
FIAT 500 1936-1972 ROAD TEST PORTFOLIO
FIAT DINO ROAD TEST PORTFOLIO
HISPANO SUIZA ROAD TEST PORTFOLIO
HONDA ST1100/ST1300 PAN EUROPEAN 1990-2002 RTP
JAGUAR MK1 & MK2 ROAD TEST PORTFOLIO
LOTUS CORTINA ROAD TEST PORTFOLIO
MV AGUSTA F4 750 & 1000 1997-2007 ROAD TEST PORTFOLIO
TATRA CARS ROAD TEST PORTFOLIO

VELOCEPRESS MOTORCYCLE BOOKS & MANUALS

1930'S BRITISH MOTORCYCLE CARBS & ELEC COMPONENTS (BOOK OF)
1930'S BRITISH MOTORCYCLE GEARBOXES & CLUTCHES (BOOK OF)
AJS SINGLES & TWINS 250cc THRU 1000cc 1932-1948 (BOOK OF)
AJS SINGLES 1955-65 350cc & 500cc (BOOK OF)
AJS SINGLES 1945-60 350cc & 500cc MODELS 16 & 18 (BOOK OF)
ARIEL 1939-1960 4 STROKE SINGLES (BOOK OF)
ARIEL LEADER & ARROW 1958-1964 (BOOK OF)
ARIEL MOTORCYCLES 1933-1951 WSM
ARIEL PREWAR MODELS 1932-1939 (BOOK OF)
BMW M/CYCLES R26 R27 (1956-1967) FACTORY WSM
BMW M/CYCLES R50 R50S R60 R69S (1955-1969) FACTORY WSM
BSA BANTAM ALL MODELS FROM 1948 ONWARDS (BOOK OF)
BSA SINGLES & V-TWINS UP TO 1927 (BOOK OF)
BSA SINGLES & V-TWINS UP TO 1935 (BOOK OF)
BSA SINGLES & V-TWINS 1936-1939 (BOOK OF)
BSA SINGLES & V-TWINS 1936-1952 (BOOK OF)
BSA OHV & SV SINGLES 250-600cc 1945-1954 (BOOK OF)
BSA OHV & SV SINGLES - 250cc 1954-1970 (BOOK OF)
BSA OHV SINGLES 350 & 500cc 1955-1967 (BOOK OF)
BSA TWINS 1948-1962 (BOOK OF)
BSA TWINS 1962-1969 (SECOND BOOK OF)
CATALOG OF BRITISH MOTORCYCLES (1951 MODELS)
DOUGLAS PRE-WAR ALL MODELS 1929-1939 (BOOK OF)
DOUGLAS POST-WAR ALL MODELS 1948-1957 FACTORY WSM
DUCATI 160cc, 250cc & 350cc OHC MODELS FACTORY WSM
HONDA 50 ALL MODELS UP TO 1970 INC MONKEY & TRAIL (BOOK OF)
HONDA 90 ALL MODELS UP TO 1966 (BOOK OF)
HONDA MOTORCYCLES 125-150 TWINS C/CS/CB/CA WSM
HONDA MOTORCYCLES 250-305 TWINS C/CS/CB WSM
HONDA MOTORCYCLES C100 SUPER CUB WSM
HONDA MOTORCYCLES C110 SPORT CUB 1962-1969 WSM
HONDA TWINS & SINGLES 50cc THRU 305cc 1960-1966 (BOOK OF)
HONDA TWINS ALL MODELS 125cc THRU 450cc UP TO 1968 (BOOK OF)
INDIAN PONYBIKE, BOY RACER & PAPOOSE ILL PARTS LIST & SALES LIT
J.A.P. ENGINES 1927-1952 & MOTORCYCLES 1934-1952 (BOOK OF)
LAMBRETTA ALL 125 & 150cc MODELS 1947-1957 (BOOK OF)
LAMBRETTA LI & TV MODELS 1957-1970 (SECOND BOOK OF)
MATCHLESS 350 & 500cc SINGLES 1945-1956 (BOOK OF)
MATCHLESS 350 & 500cc SINGLES 1955-1966 (BOOK OF)
MOTORCYCLE ENGINEERING (P. E. Irving)
NORTON 1932-1947 (BOOK OF)
NORTON 1938-1956 (BOOK OF)
NORTON DOMINATOR TWINS 1955-1965 (BOOK OF)
NORTON MODELS 19, 50 & ES2 1955-1963 (BOOK OF)
NORTON MOTORCYCLES 1957-1970 FACTORY WSM
NORTON PREWAR MODELS 1932-1939 (BOOK OF)
NSU PRIMA ALL MODELS 1956-1964 (BOOK OF)
NSU QUICKLY ALL MODELS 1953-1963 (BOOK OF)
RALEIGH MOPEDS 1960-1969 (BOOK OF)
RALEIGH MOTORCYCLES 1919-1933 (BOOK OF)
ROYAL ENFIELD SINGLES & V TWINS 1934-1946 (BOOK OF)
ROYAL ENFIELD SINGLES & V TWINS 1937-1953 (BOOK OF)
ROYAL ENFIELD SINGLES 1946-1962 (BOOK OF)
ROYAL ENFIELD 736cc INTERCEPTOR FACTORY WSM
ROYAL ENFIELD 250cc & 350cc SINGLES 1958-1966 (SECOND BOOK OF)
RUDGE MOTORCYCLES 1933-1939 (BOOK OF)
SPEED AND HOW TO OBTAIN IT
SUNBEAM MOTORCYCLES 1928-1939 (BOOK OF)
SUNBEAM S7 & S8 1946-1957 (BOOK OF)
SUZUKI 50cc & 80cc UP TO 1966 (BOOK OF)
SUZUKI T10 1963-1967 FACTORY WSM
SUZUKI T20 & T200 1965-1969 FACTORY WSM
TRIUMPH PRE-WAR MOTORCYCLE 1935-1939 (BOOK OF)
TRIUMPH MOTORCYCLES 1935-1949 (BOOK OF)
TRIUMPH MOTORCYCLES 1937-1951 WSM
TRIUMPH MOTORCYCLES 1945-1955 FACTORY WSM
TRIUMPH TWINS 1945-1958 (BOOK OF)
TRIUMPH TWINS 1956-1969 (BOOK OF)
VELOCETTE ALL SINGLES & TWINS 1925-1970 (BOOK OF)
VESPA 1951-1961 (BOOK OF)
VESPA 125 & 150cc & GS MODELS 1955-1963 (SECOND BOOK OF)
VESPA 90, 125 & 150cc 1963-1972 (THIRD BOOK OF)
VESPA GS & SS 1955-1968 (BOOK OF)
VILLIERS ENGINE UP TO 1959 INC. 3 WHEELERS (BOOK OF)
VILLIERS ENGINE UP TO 1969 (BOOK OF)
VINCENT MOTORCYCLES 1935-1955 WSM

For a detailed description of any title above please visit our website: www.VelocePress.com

Please check our website:

www.VelocePress.com

for a complete up-to-date list of available titles

www.ingramcontent.com/pod-product-compliance
Lightning Source LLC
Chambersburg PA
CBHW070550170426
43201CB00012B/1789